Endc

(in addition to those

Dr. Callen speaks the truth with love, providing solid background of the Church of God Movement's history and the highs and lows of her 140-year saga. He poses serious questions and challenges the church to stay true to the original message which gave her birth.

Robert L. Moss, Executive at Church of God Ministries and
Senior Pastor of Hope Community Church, Niles, Michigan

Dr. Callen has written dozens of books, but this is his best. We MUST follow his lead and take a hard and honest look at where we have been and where we are as a Movement, and then take the risks necessary to move forward.

Ann Smith, beloved Asian missionary of the Church of God and
respected voice of wisdom in her long retirement

Dr. Callen is gifted at stimulating needed dialogue by pulling together a pre-ferred future for the Church of God. Allow this book to bring focus to a renewed ministry.

Dr. Ronald V. Duncan, General Director Emeritus of Church of God
Ministries and Executive Director of the Global Wesleyan Alliance

Here is a solid review of the Movement's history, gracefully pointing out strengths and weaknesses, good decisions and some mis-steps along the way. It's Callen's correct contention that key aspects of this reform heritage can serve as dependable guides for impacting today's world with the resources of the king-dom of God.

Darryl O. Allen, Advancement Director, Church of God Ministries and
Senior Pastor of Dayspring Community Church, McMinnville, TN

Does the Church of God Movement have a future? The answer depends on whether we are willing to talk seriously, openly, and vulnerably about the ques-tions and responses that Barry Callen raises and gives in this helpful book.

Arthur M. Kelly, professor, Warner Pacific and Anderson Universities,
former Director of the SHAPE program of the Church of God

Barry Callen has constructed an accurate verbal picture of the Church of God Movement, including its attractiveness and blemishes. This is the necessary starting-point for contemporaries who hope to chart the Movement's future.

Donald L. Collins, Pastor Emeritus
Park Place Church of God, Anderson, Indiana

I really enjoyed the book and its call to something new. We need to connect with younger pastors. We need new language for key theological words and concepts. There's a great effort here.

M. Andrew Gale, Executive Director, Global Strategy, Church of God Ministries, Anderson, Indiana

I hope this book will enjoy wide circulation and attention. I especially appreciate the questions at the end of each chapter and can see local congregations diving deep into these critical issues.

John H. Aukerman, former Editor of the *Newsletter* and current editor of the Facebook page of the Church of God Historical Society, longtime professor of Christian Education at Anderson School of Theology

Is the Church of God Movement relevant today or has it's distinctiveness eroded over time? This important question is explored in these insightful and engaging pages. Critical information provides the basis for a much-needed conversation as the Movement seeks to understand itself and its role in today's rapidly-changing world.

J. David Reames, longtime Church of God pastor, missionary, and missions administrator

Dr. Callen asks some painful yet necessary questions. His book advances a crucial dialogue in which Church of God people must seek and find a more faithful way to fulfill the Lord's calling in our time. I hope every reader will enter actively into this conversation.

Joe Allison, former Warner Press Director of Discipleship Resources and Curriculum

It's my honor to recommend this book to those who wish greater understanding of the journey taken by the Church of God Movement. Identified are key issues that the Movement must work through in order to claim future territory that God wants to give. A must read for anyone desiring a preferable future for this wonderful Christian family.

Dr. Robert W. Pearson, First General Director of Church of God Ministries

Thank you, Dr. Callen, for writing such an important book for the Church of God, reflecting on who we have been, are, and still can be. I love the Church of God and believe her time again has come to help heal and bring about unity in the Body of Christ. This honest evaluation will help make it so. We are the messengers of reconciliation!

Mark Shaner, longtime Church of God pastor, Southeast
Regional Coordinator, National Network of Youth Ministries

Every Christian has a legacy in every other Christian. We receive that legacy only as we receive each other and relate, moving eagerly beyond group boundaries. We must re-examine the boundaries imposed by denominational differences and distinctions in the attempt to understand and live out the imperatives of Christian unity.

—James Earl Massey, *Views from the Mountain*, p. 202.

B. E. Warren, D. S. Warner, Nannie Kigar, Sarah Smith & Frances Warner

FORWARD, EVER FORWARD!

The Church of God Movement Yesterday and Tomorrow

Barry L. Callen

Mid-America Christian
University Press

ANDERSON
UNIVERSITY
PRESS

EMETH PRESS
www.emethpress.com

Forward, Ever Forward! The Church of God Movement
Yesterday and Tomorrow

Library of Congress Cataloging-in-Publication Data

Names: Callen, Barry L., author.
　Title: Forward, ever forward! : the Church of God movement yesterday and tomorrow / Barry L. Callen.
Description: Lexington, Kentucky : Emeth Press, 2020. | Includes bibliographical references. | Summary: "This book reviews the life journey of the Church of God Movement that began in the social and church worlds of the 1880s, worlds very different from those today. It then submits that world of yesterday to a serious contemporary check-up, and points to changes necessary if the Movement is to have a meaningful future, maybe any future"-- Provided by publisher.
Identifiers: LCCN 2020014214 (print) | LCCN 2020014215 (ebook) | ISBN 9781609471545 (paperback) | ISBN 9781609471552 (kindle edition)
Subjects: LCSH: Church of God (Anderson, Ind.)--History--20th century. | Church of God (Anderson, Ind.)--History--21st century.
Classification: LCC BX7025 .C345 2020 (print) | LCC BX7025 (ebook) | DDC 286.7/3--dc23
LC record available at https://lccn.loc.gov/2020014214

THE ONGOING PILGRIMAGE OF THE CHURCH OF GOD MOVEMENT

PREFACE

I admit that on occasion I have encouraged a rumor. A secret recording recently was found. It captures the frantic conversation between Adam and Eve as they were being forced from the Garden for their disobedience. At one point, Adam is overheard saying, "Honey, we're living in changing times!"

Indeed they were, and most who have come and gone ever since have thought they were too. And so do we today, and with good reason. Our societies, institutions, and faith communities are in considerable flux. The Church of God Movement is no exception.

Twenty years ago, my dear friend Gilbert W. Stafford released the book *Church of God at the Crossroads*. His concern about this Christian reform body was real, and it's even more real today. The Movement in North America now ordains an average of 135 young ministers each year. Many of them bring limited personal history with this Movement. They tend to have more interest in getting established in ministry than in understanding and furthering the particular goals of the larger Movement of which they are becoming new leaders.

On the other end of their ministerial careers is the large body of retirees who have seen much change in recent years and occasionally admit that, to their own shock, "I'm not sure if I care where the Church of God Movement goes anymore!" They carry confusion and mixed feelings about all the change.

There's more difficulty being faced than internal erosion of "denominational" awareness and support. Recent decades have seen the rise of "post-Christian" societies, especially in North America and Europe. This new mind-set is seriously eroding the popularity, stability, and social influence of the Christian faith and its institutions. These no longer are being held in high esteem .nor widely judged to be culturally relevant. Most Christian bodies are scrambling to adjust, many with little success.

Again, the Church of God Movement is no exception. And for this Movement, there's yet another complicating factor. Christian reform bodies experience lifecycles. Many observers are judging that this particular Movement is showing signs of being well beyond its middle age. It's even in danger of actual death in another generation or two unless it has a serious check-up and makes a few critical life changes. Hardly welcomed by many is still more change!

I view myself as now playing a role similar to that of the Movement's Charles E. Brown in the 1930s, 1940s, and 1950s. He was loyal to the Church of God Movement without being blind to the datedness of some of the thought of its pioneers. Brown emerged as a vital link between the popular thought of the early Movement and what he judged historically and theologically more responsible for later times. I seek to be such a vital link in today's very different times.

Brown's generation was coming to realize that the Movement was not a completely new or necessarily the final phase of God's plan for reforming a failed church before Christ's return. As I noted in my Foreword to a recent edition of Brown's classic *The Meaning of Sanctification*: "Holiness reformation was an ancient theme in church history. It had flowed for centuries, creating valleys now being traveled by this Movement. Brown saw and honored both these valleys and the Movement he had come to see backlit with their ancient wisdom."[1] He was humbled and encouraged by this larger historical picture. Holiness reformation is an ancient and persistent instinct of the Christian community.

This book, then, is an attempt to review the life journey of the Church of God Movement that began in the social and church worlds of the 1880s, worlds very different from those today. It then submits that world of yesterday to a serious contemporary check-up, and points to changes necessary if the Movement is to have a meaningful future, maybe any future.

—Bary L. Callen, April 9, 2020

"This is a timely and much-needed book of reflections on the past, present, and daunting future journey of the Church of God Movement. It is another monumental journalistic accomplishment by one of today's most knowledgeable, gifted, and prolific authors. Dr. Barry L. Callen has thoughtfully and successfully identified challenging ways the Movement can face its new future with fresh vision and mission effectiveness."

—David L. Coolidge, Pastor of Worship and Arts Emeritus, Park Place Church of God, Anderson, Indiana

DEDICATION

The Church of God Movement has understood the church to be God's family, birthed and guided by God's gracious Spirit. The Movement has been blessed by numerous networks of human families who have been reborn into God's family and unusually gifted by the Spirit to serve the Divine family. While in debt to them all, this book is dedicated in particular to two of these wonderful human families.

In the pioneer period of the Church of God Movement, especially prominent in its ministries was the **Byrum family**, including:

Enoch E., b.1861
Noah H. (brother of Enoch), b. 1871
    Ruthven H. (son of Noah), b. 1896
Robert L., b. 1856
    Russell R. (son of Robert), b. 1888
    Bessie L. (wife of Russell), b. 1889

In the modern period of the Church of God Movement, especially prominent in its ministries has been the **Grubbs family**. They go back to Green and Mary Grubbs. To them in 1906 were born triplet boys in Troy, Alabama. Those births were in the same year that the Church of God Movement brought its offices and publishing operation to Anderson, Indiana. The numerous Church of God ministers of the Grubbs family go back to two of those three boys, J. C. and J. D. Grubbs. They include:

J. C. Grubbs, b. 1906 (twin brother of J. D.)
    Dwight L. (son of J. C.), b. 1933
    Sylvia K. (wife of Dwight), b. 1940
        Jonathan D. (son of Dwight and Sylvia), b. 1966
            Hannah Oeschle (daughter of Jonathan), b. 1994
    Laura Maxine (daughter of J. C.), b. 1937
    Jerry C. (son of J. C.), b. 1940
    J. Perry (son of J. C.), b. 1941
        Reagan S. (son of Perry), b. 1968

J. D. Grubbs, b. 1906 (twin brother of J. C.)
    R. Dale (son of J. D.), b. 1931
    Mable (daughter of J. D.), b. 1933
        Greg D. Prather (son of Mable), b. 1960
    J. David (son of J. D.), b. 1935
        Martin D. (son of David), b. 1959
            Kristin Elizabeth Grubbs, b. 1989
            Cole Martin Grubbs, b. 1993

The Byrum and Grubbs families, yielding so many outstanding church leaders, contributed in numerous ways to the early formation and continuing ministries of the Church of God Movement. For their great gifts and exemplary faithfulness, I say, as they all would say, **to God be the glory**!

A Brief Roadmap of a Movement's Ongoing Journey

I was completing this manuscript in early 2020. The news was full of suggested bits of wisdom about life in a time of transition. One reporter said, "There are two kinds of people, those who romanticize the past and those who yearn for an entirely new future." I attempt here to avoid being either. I happily honor the past but do so carefully enough not to merely romanticize it. In these very different times, I yearn for a fresh future, one that I know can't be quite like the past. As the Church of God Movement heads *forward, ever forward!*, its tomorrow must be open to change while staying rooted in much that was truly good yesterday—and much good there indeed has been.

The following is a quick overview of this book's manner of navigating this delicate but essential path from yesterday to tomorrow. It traces the book's broad outline of a special people still traveling toward a land believed to be promised by God. This people soon became known as the Church of God Movement, with the word "Reformation" sometimes placed before "Movement." For more than a century, the phrase "Anderson, Indiana" often was added as well.

This special body of Christian people now faces a circumstance being faced by many church bodies. "Just as an organism must adapt in order to thrive in a changing environment, so organizations need to adapt to the changing world around them without losing their core identities, their reason for being, their core values and purpose."[2] Our quest here, then, is to identify the core identity, values, and purposes of the Church of God Movement and go on to explore the adaptations now being required by this changing world.

The intended destiny of this Movement is to become a holy and united people of God that is successful in helping to prepare the whole Bride of Christ, the church, to be all she's intended to be. The Movement's journey so far has been one of vision, joy, excitement, and courage, and also one that has experienced frustration, failed experiments, and constant opposition from various enemies. It's not easy being God's people in this fallen world, especially being a "reformation movement" that's determined to be and stimulate in others all that God desires.

I firmly believe that the divine journey of this special people is not over. However, the next stage of its life requires careful reassessment of direction, assumptions, motives, methods, and proper traveling companions. These pages attempt such reassessment and hope to raise the right questions and present at least a few of the necessary answers. They hope to provide a record of the journey to date that will inform and stimulate today's travelers to think seriously about where they now are, how they got here, and where they should be going next. The book's success will be measured in large part by whether or not it stimulates critical conversations that result in needed actions.

Following is initial help for the reader. It's the book's design that highlights the reasoning behind the sequence of chapters, as well as their individual emphases. Note the obvious parallels with the journey of the ancient Jews as they were freed from Egypt and traveled through the desert for decades, seeking God's promised land. The biblical record is a primary guide for God's people who still are seeking the church's promised land.

Note also the critical biblical transition found between chapters four and five. It features the ancient people of God having returned to Jerusalem after a long and difficult exile. With a new future believed to be still ahead, the critical question was how should they rebuild, how they should honor the past without failing to recognize the fresh challenges and thus the new ways required to claim the wonderful promises of God. That's exactly where the Church of God Movement now finds itself.

Chapter 1—We begin where the Movement is now. This is a critical time in its life journey. She must not wait until some later time to hold up a mirror, see where the journey has brought her to date, and be honest about what the mirror shows and recommends next. Three unacceptable current options are refusing to look in the mirror, looking but denying what is seen, or seeing what's real and now needed but doing nothing about it.

Chapter 2—To know herself well, the Movement has the privilege of first remembering the powerful vision that launched this amazing church-reformation journey. What assumptions and motivations were once exciting and strong enough to explain how this major journey got started? Movement pioneers knew themselves to be called by God to "come out" of the church's bondage, be free in the Spirit, and begin a divine journey to a better land. In their view, the Bible predicted this very reformation development.

Chapter 3—The Movement's journey forward, however, soon encountered really rough ground. Some of the key launching assumptions failed to stand the test of time. By the 1920s, unpleasant realities had begun to force changes in direction that were confusing and even painful. Key leaders began to rethink aspects of the early vision that launched the journey. They had to decide how to adjust to the new territory being encountered. At various points, the traveling adjustments were as awkward and unwelcome as they appeared necessary.

Chapter 4—Early idealisms soon clashed with surrounding realities. The daily life of the church's travelers became caught in troubling paradoxes. From at least the 1920s clear to the present day, the Movement was increasingly functioning in ways that at times seemed at odds with its own cherished beliefs about its own original nature and calling. Its progress occasionally seemed like going in circles, and often through one dangerous valley after another. Some leaders even wondered if they should turn around and go back to the old bondage rather than go into more compromising territory.

But there would be no giving up, only the struggle of finding the best way forward. Some Movement leaders in the early years of the twentieth century began the process of founding church institutions within the Movement's life. Was this the natural fulfillment or the abandonment of its reforming idealisms? More fresh institutional beginnings have been occurring in the early years of the twenty-first century, along with the persistent questions about their legitimacy.

A Biblical Transition. There finally has arrived this present time, similar to the one faced by the ancient Jews after their release from a long Exile. It's a crucial time to pause and consider carefully. Since at least the 1950s, the Church of God Movement has been experiencing what was faced by the Jews when they returned to Jerusalem from exile in Babylon. What should they do now? The beloved yesterday lay in shambles. Should they rebuild Jerusalem as it was before the exile and try to be God's people as they were before that terrible time of judgment? What did God want for his people in such a new time?

It was a biblical transition time much like what is being faced today by the Church of God Movement. The vision reported in Zechariah 2 should have been followed then and also now by today's Movement. The Movement may not be in shambles, and in some ways is even flourishing, but many things are very different than they were much earlier in its journey. Some trends clearly are threatening its future effectiveness and maybe even existence. The Zechariah 2 vision is still a word from God for today.

The Movement is now well into its long journey. Key directional decisions are urgently required. Times of judgment have been experienced. What vision for the path ahead will be seen and followed? The transition now faced is moving from remembering yesterday to rebuilding for tomorrow. Accordingly, the remaining chapters of this book identify key points of needed decision and offer at least beginning suggestions about the best ways to go. The first subject to be addressed is the matter of determining proper authority in church life. The other subjects naturally follow.

Chapter 5—Given the past generations of vision, beliefs, tensions, change, and a possible new beginning, what now must be especially re-thought, restructured, and redirected? What's required if the Movement is to continue being God-inspired, enduring, and relevant to the present and soon-coming days? The first correctional guide for tomorrow's leg of the Movement's journey is to understand properly the relationships among the Bible, the spiritual experience of believers, and the resulting approach to forming Christian doctrine.

These three core aspects of Christian faith and life have been central in the history of the Movement, but they have not always been understood properly or kept in proper relation to each other. There is particular concern today about the classic Movement slogan, "the Bible is our only creed." How can this have continued meaning when recent generations of the Movement are nearly as biblically illiterate as the society as a whole? Studied biblical exposition is rarely heard from Movement pulpits.

Chapter 6—Beliefs are the backbone of any church body. The Movement always has been a convictional body, believing deeply and proclaiming widely. However, it also has been strongly opposed to formalizing its beliefs into mandatory creedal statements "like the denominations do." There have been good reasons for this stance, and it's brought a sense of freedom and flexibility in the fellowship. But it also has encouraged a subtle doctrinal paralysis that threatens to be an open door to nearly any passing wind of current thought. The theological identity of today's Movement must move beyond merely insisting that it's an anti-creedal body. More doctrinal backbone than that is needed at this stage of the journey.

Chapter 7—Once the fundamental matters of church authority and doctrinal stance are settled, the next step for today's Movement is determining what the larger body of Christ needs today and what the Movement possesses in its tradition that can address that need helpfully. The Movement always has understood itself to be a "reform" body called to address the pressing need of the entire fellowship of believers in Jesus. At first it saw the need being to denounce the accumulated compromise of the churches and the destructive weight of "denominationalism." In this new time, the need of the global church must be newly identified and then the Movement's own tradition and current reviewed. What theological resources might it have that could be shared for the good of the larger church? Once identified, the Movement must find the courage to step out of the shadows of the larger church's life, where it has tended to live, and actively share with others, while also humbly receiving back from them.

Chapter 8—The Movement always has believed that the church in any age needs two critical things. It needs within its ranks the renewing experience of holiness, the full integrity of transformed new life in God's Spirit. It then needs the healing of that holiness reality to be activated into encouraging a Spirit-unity within the larger church. This is all believed to be necessary for an abundant Christian life and a healthy church with a witness to the world that is credible and effective. Holiness comes first. The Movement today must reclaim this fundamental spiritual reality of "holiness," newly understand what it really is, and freshly commit to its personal and congregational realizations. The original keynote of the Movement was proclaiming and experiencing Christian holiness. The Movement's ongoing journey with a holy God now calls for, requires, and makes possible nothing less.

Chapter 9—If Christian holiness is reclaimed and truly experienced by members of today's Movement, there should be two essential and natural outcomes. First, there should be a God-enabled unity within its own fellowship that transcends the race, gender, and the other human barriers that block true unity in Christ. Second, its unified fellowship should come to function as a unifying bridge church-wide that replaces the destructive tendency of believers to build dividing walls between themselves and others. Holiness is the key to true Christian unity. This key is urgently needed as the church today seeks to minister in a severely divided world.

Preaching and teaching about Christian holiness was constant in the early decades of the Movement's journey. Such an emphasis must return, although understandings of the meaning and lifestyle implications of holiness may not be the same as before. The Movement must also address the continuing dividedness within its own ranks, a quiet scandal undercutting effective witness to the unifying power of life in Christ.

Chapter 10—The Movement is highly sensitive to the downsides of humans burdening the church with their self-seeking organizations. However, the Movement has suffered from the downsides of failing to structure church life for the maximum use of the spiritual gifts made available to it by God. If the church is a family, a living "organism," how can it be organized for effective mission without compromising its very nature? Being a holy body that cares deeply about Christian unity will never be adequate for having widespread impact on the church as a whole.

Beyond caring for a lost world must be the developing of specific strategic initiatives supported by careful planning and some manner of reasonable coordination of effort. The Movement has struggled with an organizational dilemma since its beginning. It has seen clearly the dangers of "human" organization in the church's life, and yet also has slowly come to realize that the benefits of some structures of mutual accountability are very much needed. A meaningful middle ground must be found if progress is to be real.

Chapter 11—Once there is in place some workable pattern of careful planning supported by a reasonable coordination of effort, the issue becomes one of identifying what strategic initiatives to take. What is the church's mission goal, the "main thing" of its very life. The Movement has thought of itself as a "Reformation" Movement called of God to re-lease the church from its compromises and bring it back to God's inten-tion. Should such church reform still be the primary focus of the Movement? If so, it now must consider the new and difficult task of first reforming *itself*. It no longer lives free of the dilemmas that other church bodies have long faced. What then about evangelism? Isn't it the main thing for church mission, not internal focus on church reform? Isn't world evangelism the central commission given by Jesus to his disciples? The proper evangelism-reformation balance must be found.

Chapter 12—According to the New Testament, evangelism is indeed the main thing. Church reform is sometimes necessary so that God's family can be freed to focus on its real mission. There is great good news in Christ and it's to be shared. Heaven is the goal of Christian faith, *but not the only goal*. The fruit of saving faith must not be kept at the personal level. The Movement's understanding always has been that believers, once renewed in Christ, are to be faithful *in the meantime*, faithful in min-istering *now* on the way to God's eventual *then*.

Many early pioneers of the Movement expected Christ's return in their own lifetimes. That didn't happen. But they also believed that God's reign already has arrived in Jesus. That arrival is to be evidenced and activated by the people of Jesus in the midst of the current realities of this world. Salvation is both *from* sin and *to* life engagement that seeks salvation, healing, and justice for others. God's kingdom that is assured for tomorrow is to be the church's agenda today. Speculation about end times must not be allowed to distract from ministry to the present time.

Chapter 13—A "movement" that isn't moving, changing, adapting, and rethinking its identity and role is *ceasing to be a movement*. It's stag-nating and becoming only another denominational body in the mix of many others. Is that the eventual fate of the Church of God Movement? What could Movement leaders be doing today to avoid such a sad out-come of their long pilgrimage toward God's promised land? The Move-ment now must be very vigilant in this regard or it will wind up back in bondage where its journey began.

Important Volume Note: This journey of the Church of God Move-ment is reported frankly in these pages, always acknowledging victories and failures and exhibiting a willingness to face important questions needing careful and maybe answers today. The suggested path ahead includes some refinements on past positions and strategies of the Movement, but it never ranges outside the established guidelines put in place over the decades by the General Assembly of the Church of God (United States and Canada). These guidelines are the Movement's best thinking by its most representative voice. They are honored in these pages and can be found in the volume *Leaning Forward!* (Barry L. Callen, ed., 2019).

Chapter
I

TIME FOR THE
WHOLE TRUTH

The Church of God Movement now needs to hold up a mirror, look into it honestly, recall its journey to date, and face frankly its past problems and future challenges. Failing to do this risks ceasing to be a meaningful instrument of God today. And today is in desperate need of the fresh moving of God!

A scattered group of visionary Christians back in the 1880s faced a time when the church was compromised and not addressing well a rapidly-changing culture. These visionaries sensed a divine call to do something about this and soon gathered into what became the Church of God Movement. This reforming body now has nearly a century and a half of its own life behind it. It has impacted for good numerous church leaders from a range of church bodies across the generations. It also has reached a point when it must review where it is, what it is, and what's next for its ongoing existence.

In some ways this historic process now has begun repeating itself. A small group of visionary Christian leaders first met in 2003 and soon formed what's now known as the *Wesleyan Holiness Connection*. In only sixteen years of existence, this WHC has impacted for good numerous of today's Christian leaders from a range of church bodies in the Wesleyan-Holiness Christian tradition, the very one out of which the Church of God Movement emerged. The goal has been similar, this time seeking to address the "secularized" state of today's North American culture by challenging and resourcing a weakened and compromised church.

So much has changed since the 1880s, and some things haven't improved much at all. The very rise of the WHC suggests that the mission of the Church of God Movement is far from complete. It also suggests that today the Movement needs allies in the task and a willingness to examine carefully its calling in a very new time. I have been privileged to represent the Church of God Movement in the *Wesleyan Holiness Connection* since its beginning. As an ordained minister of this Movement, I hope to assist with its needed reexamination.

A Modern Manifesto

By 2006 the WHC had determined to state today's problem clearly and broadcast it widely. I quote a few lines because it describes well the context of today's Church of God Movement. Known as *The Holiness Manifesto*, it begins:

> There has never been a time in greater need of a compelling articulation of the message of holiness. Pastors and church leaders at every level of the church have come to new heights of frustration in seeking ways to revitalize their congregations and denominations. Membership in churches of all traditions has flat-lined at best. The power and health of churches have also been drained by the incessant search for a better method, a more effective fad, a newer and bigger program to yield growth. In the process of trying to lead growing, vibrant churches, our people have become largely ineffective and fallen prey to a generic Christianity that results in congregations that are indistinguishable from the culture around them.

Another way of stating the great need of the 1880s, and now of our time as well, is trumpeting the call "to a dangerous oddness." Walter Brueggemann says that "we either sign on uncritically to the powers that surround us or we take on the prophetic task of exposing the contradictions and performing the alternatives."[3] The Church of God Movement and now the WHC have embraced the "dangerous oddness" and assumed the "prophetic task."

For many generations now, leaders of the Church of God Movement have been glad to announce the idealism of their vision of needed church reform. Less often, however, have they been equally clear about the downsides of their own attempted implementation of the envisioned reform. Altering wayward church life is difficult and an ongoing process. It requires more than criticizing the failures of others. The Movement now must dare to look closely at itself, especially in the context of its current social setting.

Having the vision of God's will for the church and facing honestly the challenges of its implementation are both necessary if adequate reform is to move forward. Church reformers must be idealistic and realistic. The resulting tension forces an examination of the journey of the Church of God Movement to date and the identification of the dangerous drifts that have weakened its "dangerous oddness" and undercut its prophetic task. Is there anything now placing the Movement in danger of getting off course and failing to be able to impact the dilemmas of today with the good news of God in Jesus Christ?

The Movement, especially in its early years in the late nineteenth century, judged most other Christians as arrogant "sectarians" tragically dividing the church and undercutting its world mission. The Movement, however, didn't work hard at building up its own congregations and refused at first to establish its own church institutions—which it tended to judge a joining of the "apostasy" of the church in general.

Instead, the Movement initially focused on what it understood to be its commission, bringing the fruit of holiness, and the unity it should enable, to the entire Christian world, and to do so quickly before the soon return of Christ. However, this mission often was announced and implemented harshly. The Movement tended to judge others for their glaring failures and isolate itself from them if they did not respond acceptably. There was more tearing down than building up. The time for this is now gone!

It's Now Time!

Time provides perspective not available to the original pioneers of the Church of God Movement. Now the time has come to examine the whole truth about the Movement itself, not just the admirable and comfortable parts—of which there are many. We intend in these pages to attempt an exploration of the whole truth, knowing that much of it is exciting and joyous, while some of it is frustrating and troubling.

Frank assessments help enable future accomplishments. Church of God people have dreamed great dreams and now also must face what's real and possible. Has the Movement been criticizing in vain the weaknesses of other church bodies while turning a blind eye toward its own? What has it accomplished? What has gone well, what hasn't, and what's best to do next? When holding up a mirror today, what does the Movement see?

The Church of God Movement has tended to be a daring body of truth-tellers about the failures of the denominational world. I now invite an exploration of the successes and failures of the Movement, highlighting its twists and turns over the generations. Movements cannot continue to move in the right direction unless they face the full truth about themselves, both the considerable good and the sometimes not so good.

To be faithful as a movement of God means that it will dare to keep open to needed church reform, even reform of itself. The Movement must keep moving. Russell R. Byrum, beloved theologian-writer-educator of the Movement, posed the proper questions in 1928:

> Did God give to the Church of God Reformation Movement the whole truth fifty years ago, or may the Spirit give us fuller light now? Do we have a creed other than the Bible—formal or informal, written or unwritten—which binds us to the views of the past, or which prevents our receiving clearer light?[4]

These are critical questions indeed. There's a tendency for a church reform movement to be overly tied to its own past and reluctant to allow God's Spirit the freedom to forge for it a fresh future. Such reluctance is at odds with what the Church of God Movement is all about. It must not allow itself to be tied too tightly to its own yesterdays.

I share Byrum's hope that the Spirit of God will show this Movement a fresh light, a brighter light for today, the best path toward fulfilling in this time the mission of God's people. I want this Movement to be at the forefront of God's activity today, to be passionate forerunners of the change needed now, as D. S. Warner, Mary Cole, E. E. Byrum, Bessie Byrum, F. G. Smith, E. A. Reardon, Nora Hunter, and the other pioneers of this Movement were in their times and places.

To be on the forefront of needed change requires four important things: (1) to know and appreciate the Church of God Movement's rich history; (2) to boldly acknowledge where the Movement's journey might have become more drift sideways than surge forward; (3) to avoid holding so tightly to all the particulars of the Movement's past thinking and acting that the Movement "sectarianizes" and stagnates itself, obstructing participation in God's ongoing work; and (4) to examine the Word of God to ensure that any changes made are aligned with Scripture and the leading of God's Spirit.

All Voices Welcome

Others have stepped forward to examine the whole truth about the Church of God Movement in their various times. Albert F. Gray properly posed this key question in 1950: "Was this Movement, in its fundamental aspects, as established by our early brethren, the work of God, or was it the result of a misdirected zeal?"[5] We seek to answer this question as carefully and fairly as we can, convinced with Gray that the answer is "both." Much has been from God, although it has been mixed with some inevitable human elements.

Gray went on in 1950 to honor God's work through this Movement from its very beginning, but he also criticized "the excesses that existed among our early brethren."[6] He affirmed that such criticism is "just what they would do if they were still alive. It was always their expressed intention to walk in clearer light as it comes." If the Movement ignores what has stagnated in its own life, only pointing uncritically to past accomplishments and idealized goals, it will cease its moving and fossilize into the denominational mire it has criticized so vigorously.

Examining the whole truth requires that we silence no voice. I have listened carefully to H. M. Riggle, E. A. Reardon, Russell R. Byrum, Albert F. Gray, Charles Naylor, Val Clear, John W. V. Smith, Gilbert W. Stafford, James Earl Massey, and many more who have spoken wisely in the past (see the bibliography, many consultants, and numerous endnotes at the end of this book). Let's open the forgotten file cabinets, pull out of storage the dusty reports, and take seriously the outcomes of some of the Movement's major self-studies and wisest thinkers of yesterday.

Let's hear well the studied insights of our historians Charles E. Brown, John W. V. Smith, and Merle D. Strege. Let's honor appropriately our primary pioneer, Daniel S. Warner, and also be careful not to repeat any aspect of his teaching that has not stood well the test of time. Let's long for the truth that fired Warner's soul, but without trying to resurrect any cold ashes of that fire's burning in very different times.

Does the Movement have all the answers? No. Does it believe it's the only body that sees things clearly? I hope not. The love for God's true church creates a fire in our bones to seek clarity, holiness, and unity with all Christian brothers and sisters. We always should be anxious to relight the fires of revelation and reformation as God enables them in our time!

"Coming Out" Again

The Movement's earliest generations were "come-outers."[7] They were a nineteenth-century burst of church-reforming idealists and activists. Many things were wrong with the church bodies the Movement pioneers encountered, and the pioneers dared to "come out" into the brighter light of how they judged things ought to be. It was messy, conflicted, only beginning steps, but it was daring, Spirit-enthused, and productive in many ways.

These pioneers of yesterday had no intention of starting a new church organization. Rather, they intended to spearhead the final activities of God before the return of Christ. They hoped to stimulate the gathering of "the saints" out of "sectism" and thus realize the ideal of God's purified and united church. It was believed that this "last reformation" soon would envelop the entire Body of Christ. Daniel Warner, the primary pioneer of the Movement, was sure that Jesus was going to return during his lifetime to claim the Bride, the true and waiting church. She had to be gotten ready!

Warner died in 1895. Christ is yet to return much more than a century later. Idealists must come to be realists. The full preparation of the Bride of Christ has hardly happened yet. The Church of God Movement is now left to face what it was unaware of in Warner's short lifetime, its own unexpected history of some 140 years so far. This history is full of idealism and wonderful Christian people. It's also had its share of failed experiments, frustrated expectations, and outside forces pulling it in multiple directions. These must be acknowledged and addressed openly and as fairly as possible.

I have spent my ministry loving, serving, studying, and being blessed by this particular church-reform tradition. I am thrilled by its idealism, but also saddened by various realities that have hindered its progress. I have decided to speak up, in a sense to "come out" again. This time it's not coming out from the downsides of other Christian bodies. It's re-evaluating the life of the Church of God Movement itself in the hope of assisting her readiness to address the challenges of today and tomorrow.

A prominent Christian seminary features this slogan: "The Whole Bible for the Whole World."[8] I affirm this mission as representative of the Church of God Movement at its best, adding that "Jesus Is the Subject!" The whole Bible presents to the whole world the whole truth about the presence and work of God in Jesus Christ through the Holy Spirit. It looks ahead to the glorious fulfillment of this redeeming work in our lives, in the church, and in the whole creation. To that end I dedicate these pages.

The Movement, now after its many generations, has evolved its own traditions, entrenched thought patterns, and "denominational" characteristics. It has resisted such an evolution but found necessary, and even justified as appropriate, some of what it originally criticized in others. It's time to be frank about these yesterdays on the way to a better future. Let's rejoice in this Movement's high ideals, and also dare to make needed adjustments that will keep it moving forward.

New Testament scholar William Barclay comments wisely this way on Matthew 11:11. "Let us never be discouraged in the church if a dream we have dreamed and for which we have toiled is never worked out before the end of the day. God needed John the Baptist, a signpost who could point the way, although he himself could never reach the goal."[9] The dream of the Church of God Movement is yet to be fully realized. Nevertheless, we are to be encouraged and move on, going forward, ever forward.

What Time Is It?

The years 1979-1980 were pivotal for the Church of God Movement. This was centennial time with a great celebration event staged in Anderson, Indiana. Robert H. Reardon, then president of Anderson University where the event occurred, shared this wisdom:

> It's time to ring again this great reformation bell. It's time to look long and hard at those great pillars of fire in our night which lit the way for our fathers [and mothers]. It's time to discard the old wineskins that can never take the sweet new wine of truth. It's time to break free from every trap set for us by the enemy and to climb out of every pit into which we have fallen.[10]

That's exactly what this book is about. We're checking the adequacy of the Movement's wineskins, spotting the pits of its occasional fallenness, and rejoicing in the great pillars of fire in its night.

These pillars did enable the fresh seeing of new light sent from God. They once showed the way forward and can do so again if the Movement is open to enduring truth, fresh insight, and needed change. I'm calling for that openness, and I'm guided in part by this version of a classic blessing of unknown origin but of current relevance:

> God has blessed us with a restless **discomfort**
> about easy answers, half-truths, and superficial relationships,
> so that we may seek truth boldly and love deep within our hearts.
>
> May God bless us with enough **foolishness**
> to believe that we really can make a difference,
> so that we are able, with God's grace,
> to do what others claim cannot be done.

I recount in the chapters that follow the beginning life of the Church of God Movement. Then come a series of chapters that project current growth needs and challenges. Between these two major sections is an important biblical transition. It helps us move from remembering frankly to rebuilding wisely.

There is a restless discomfort in the air that calls for change. Are you and I foolish enough to believe that, difficult or not, what is needed can and will be done? I am, and I hope you are also.

NEEDED CONVERSATION AND ACTION

1. Now is a very important time to reconsider seriously both the history and possible future of the Church of God Movement. Why do you think that's the case? Do you agree with the judgment of many concerned observers that the Movement has come to a crucial crossroads and its very future may hang in the balance?

2. Are you willing to engage openly and frankly in such a crucial reconsideration? Would you start the needed conversation with interested people around you, using this book for needed information and guidance?

3. Back in 1928, after a half-century of the Movement's life, Russell R. Byrum wondered whether God might still give to the Movement yet "fuller light" on Christian truth and mission. He was sure that the answer was "yes!" Do you think his judgment still holds for today after much more of the Movement's life has come and gone?

4. Consider again the words of Robert H. Reardon in this chapter. In their light, here's what this book's all about: "We're checking the adequacy of the Movement's wineskins, spotting the pits of its occasional fallenness, and rejoicing in the great pillars of fire in its night. These pillars once showed the way forward and can do so again if the Movement is open both to enduring truth and needed change." Are you ready to see and reject the dangerous pits and spot the flaming light that can still show the way forward?

5. Are you ready to have God bless you "with enough **foolishness** to believe that you really can make a difference?"

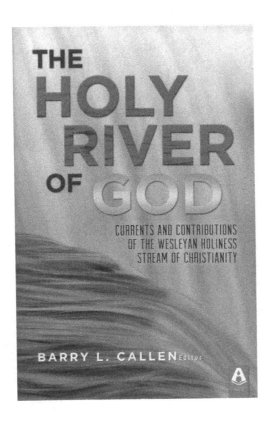

IT'S GOD'S CHURCH!

The Life & Legacy of
Daniel Sidney Warner

BARRY L. CALLEN

THE POWER OF A DRAMATIC IDENTITY

The Church of God Movement was a late nineteenth-century burst of idealism. It believed that God had commissioned this "last reformation." The church must be prepared for the soon return of Christ. It could and must be done! This understanding propelled the Movement forward.

To understand what is enduring about the Church of God Movement's place in today's church world, we must start by recalling the Movement's launching vision and understanding of its own identity and role in the larger Christian community.

What thrilled and drove forward the Movement's pioneers, as it was some others like the Christian Churches and Adventists of the time? It was a vision both dramatic and powerful. Christ was returning soon. His Bride, the church, had to be prepared by regaining her holiness and unity. Time was short and the stakes high. Articulate chart-lecturers began pointing to biblical symbols said to be picturing the exact beginning of the Church of God Movement, the instrument of God called to initiate the necessary purification. The gathering and excited saints comprising this Movement began singing lustily, "There's a mighty reformation sweeping o'er the land!"

A Burst of Spiritual Idealism

The Church of God Movement started with a personal journal entry. It pre-dated the dramatic lectures on the Book of Revelation that soon would be used to support it. Daniel S. Warner recorded this on March 7, 1878: "On the 31st of last January the Lord showed me that holiness could never prosper upon sectarian soil encumbered by human creeds and party names, and he gave me a new commission to join holiness and all truth together and build up the apostolic church of the living God." This spark soon flamed a widespread reform movement.

With this commission in hand, an inspired Warner became the primary pioneer of what soon would become the Church of God Movement.[11] Personal holiness was viewed as key from the beginning. Holiness would enable the abundant Christian life of believers and then the full unity of God's church. The supposed prophetic endorsement of this vision would soon add excitement, power, and presumed biblical affirmation.

The Movement began as a group of thrilled and determined Christian "come-outers." Many things they saw around them in the divisive denominations were judged to be seriously outside New Testament teaching and expectation. They would boldly abandon it all! These heralds of a new day, thought to be the final day of church and world history, were sure that God was calling them to do something significant on behalf of the whole church. They determined to come out, leaving entirely the unholy systems of church apostasy and abuse. They were being called to pioneer the better way ahead for God's people in the short time left before the return of Christ.

This reformation movement was an outburst of spiritual idealism.[12] It was an answering of God's call to return quickly to the apostolic "early morning time," to a church "without spot or wrinkle," to a holy life separate from "the world," to a reunion of the saved and sanctified. To be made holy by a holy God was seen as the key to becoming spiritually one with all the saints, past and present, and thus the beautifully prepared Bride of Christ.

Down with Sect Babylon!

Around 1886 this young Movement went beyond the goal of renewed holiness and began acquiring a new way of authenticating its own identity and role within the larger Holiness Movement of the time. This new way was drawn increasingly from a special manner of reading biblical prophecy. Daniel Warner, the Movement's primary pioneer, became well acquainted with the work of Uriah Smith, a leading Adventist editor and writer in Michigan.

Smith had developed an elaborate system of thought using biblical prophecy to establish the role of Adventism in God's plan for the end times. Warner at first was repelled by such self-serving use of biblical prophecy, and then he became attracted to it. If adjusted in key ways, he decided, Smith's system would serve well the Movement he and others were pioneering.[13] The adjustments made to Smith's teaching yielded the following pattern of beliefs.

The Bride of Christ (the church) was to be speedily prepared for the coming return of the Bridegroom (Christ). Christians must be called out of the "sects" into the "one body." God had forsaken Babylon, site of the Exile of the ancient Jews. That city now was being viewed as a metaphor for the centuries-long captor of the wayward church. God finally was abandoning the unholy prison of humanly devised, divisive, and apostate denominationalism.

Brother Warner and those with him had "seen the light" on the church. Now they also were seeing in the final book of the Bible the whole historical drama of that light being darkened over the centuries and now being gloriously re-ignited. They were responsible to be the heralds of this fresh light and thus bring about the church's "last reformation." There was a clear enemy of the true church and a divine commission for the Movement, just being birthed, to be on the front lines of the final battle. The Movement was propelled forward by the enthusiasm of having a great mission that had to be accomplished quickly, just before the return of Jesus and the end of time.

The Adventist Uriah Smith had drawn from biblical prophecy a "cleansing of the sanctuary" concept which presumably was beginning with his reform movement in 1844. Warner soon found himself accepting this same cleansing plan of biblical prophecy, only now applying it to the task of his young Movement of the 1880s and beyond. This reading of the Bible's "prophetic" materials began appearing in the Movement's *Gospel Trumpet* publication in 1883. Warner was now identifying the first "beast" of Revelation 13 as Roman Catholicism. The second was its Protestant daughters that separated from the first beast but carried with them its darkening disease of compromising truth and spreading unholy division.

In the April 7, 1892, issue of the *Gospel Trumpet* there appeared a large chart detailing the key dates of church history, with their biblical references, culminating in the fall of "sectism" in A. D. 1880, the traditional birthday of the Church of God Movement. Then in 1893 William Schell wrote the book *Biblical Trace of the Church* that pictures the Movement's identity as a special instrument of God prophetically called for in the end times.

This prophetic scheme was fully developed in the 1903 book *The Cleansing of the Sanctuary* by Warner and his friend H. M. Riggle (Warner had died in 1895). This book explains that there had been a moment heavy with destiny when Warner first determined that God was breaking again into history. As foretold by the prophets, the Movement being pioneered by Warner and others was being used by God to usher in the last phase of church history before the end of the age.

These courageous "come-outers" were not merely an insignificant phenomenon on the margins of the larger Holiness Movement of that time. They were understanding themselves to be heralds of the final fulfillment of God's ultimate will for the church. These pioneers were the leading edge of the "last reformation" foretold in biblical prophecy. They conveyed their self-understanding in joyous song, relying on poetry as much as prose. One song, "The Church's Jubilee" composed in 1923, captures especially well the prophetically inspired early vision and excitement.

Announces this song, "The light of even-tide now shines." God's fresh light was calling for vigorous church reform. The goal was "the darkness to dispel." What darkness was God dispelling? "For out of Babel God doth call his scattered saints in one, together all one church compose, the body of his Son." The darkness was the church's long exile in Babylon, the metaphorical place of the gathered layers of apostasy piled up across church history.

This prophetic time for the Church of God Movement was understood to be nothing less than the liberating "day of Jubilee." The church was to "rejoice and be glad." Why? Because "the Shepherd has begun his long-divided flock again to gather into one." This Movement was being called to "thrash Babylon" by challenging and abandoning all the evils of denominationalism, the sad state of the divided and apostate church. To repeat the title of a biography of Daniel Warner, "It's God's Church!"[14]

There was good news! Like Isaiah, the prophet of old, these modern Movement pioneers were witnessing Babylon's walls starting to crumble and the captivity of God's true saints coming to an end. God was about to destroy "sect Babylon" and gather the saints into the one true body of believers. The "evening light" was shining and the Movement's leaders were divinely commissioned to broadcast the great news far and wide. Here's one report of this news:

> Christ is today gathering his church out of all the sect abominations back to Zion. They return on the highway of holiness; he sanctifies and cleanses them from all sin and traditions, and thus prepares his church as "a glorious church not having spot or wrinkle or any such thing." The apostasy crushed down the church under human authority and rule, and a great pile of sectarian rubbish covered it over for centuries; but in these last days, with the flaming torch of truth, this great pile of human rubbish is being consumed and the house of God restored to its primitive glory and power.[15]

This description of the final "cleansing" of the sanctuary, the compromised church, was soon informed by a specialized reading of Scripture's "prophecies." The result thrilled and drove the Movement's early pioneers. This reading of biblical prophecy soon would be questioned by prominent Movement figures (see chapter three), leaving future generations of the Movement with a painful loss of self-identity, one that still plagues it today. From the Movement's very beginning, however, there was a more fundamental spiritual bedrock on which the Movement's earliest identity stood. It was a renewed experiencing of Christian holiness. As seen later in this book, this bedrock has never has collapsed and should remain at the Movement's center.

The Enduring Bedrock

The most fundamental bedrock of truth that always has been at the core of the Movement's identity is depicted clearly in the 1950s film *"Heaven To Earth."* It dramatizes the formative events of the Church of God Movement, with a key scene showing Daniel Warner suddenly inspired to write these poetic words:

> Fill me with Thy Spirit, Lord,
> Fully save my longing soul;
> Thro' the precious cleansing blood,
> Purify and make me whole.

> Fill me with Thy holy light,
> I would have a single eye;
> Make me perfect in Thy sight,
> Tis Thy will to sanctify.

This heart-longing of Warner filled the minds and sermons of the Movement's pioneers. They looked in their Bibles and found a beautiful church portrayed, the very body of Christ "not having spot, or wrinkle, or any such thing" (Eph. 5:27). It was to be a holy body serving a holy God.

As these pioneers looked at the "churches" about them, however, they saw so little that resembled this glorious New Testament church. They were compelled to abide in Christ alone rather than in any divisive denominational system of humans. They would seek to be filled with God's Spirit whose will it is to "sanctify."

The pioneers of the Movement were one phase of the larger Holiness Movement active in the 1870s and 1880s. While this larger Wesleyan revival sought new emphasis on personal holiness, which hopefully would renew the various denominations rooted in the Wesleyan revival of eighteenth-century England, the vision of the new reforming Movement saw a larger picture. The compromised church must itself become holy again, united outside the denominational system through the power and magnetic force of holiness.

Here is the enduring core of the originating vision of the Church of God Movement that existed prior to the overlay of supposed biblical prophecy. "Our pioneers found emphasized in their Bibles the conception of the church as a 'spiritual house' built out of the 'lively stones' of redeemed lives (1 Pet. 2:4-5). They believed in a 'gathered' church made up of those who by repentance and faith had entered into right relations with God and their fellow believers. They believed that Christ as head of his church was calling to himself a people, a new Israel, a household of God, the church of the living God."[16] True believers in the last days were to gather as the blessed holy ones, freshly united as the one family of God because of their bond of holy love.

The pioneers of this Movement were filled with spiritual excitement and a sense of liberation from centuries of human failure. They were pilgrims setting out on a holy journey. They had been freed by a vision of the dawning of God's new day for the true, holiness-formed, and thus finally unified church. This pioneer vision was that "all of the human, the partial, and the non-biblical be shed from the church's life. Believers are to stand together, unified, purified, empowered, gifted, governed, and sent by God. The church brought into being by God is to be the church *of God* and of God's agenda in the world."[17]

This grand vision gave the early Church of God Movement its identity and attractiveness, its motivation and power, and its sense of great relevance for the time. Soon this identity would become bolstered by the adding of a specialized reading of biblical prophecy. This brought extra excitement and apparent biblical support. Unfortunately, such biblical interpretation was questionable and would not stand the test of time.

A Fragile Framework

From the Movement's beginning there was believed to be time urgency—Christ would be returning very soon for his Bride, the liberated, purified, and unified church. This urgency became fired further by a presumed biblical framework of prophecy that provided a comprehensive understanding of all church history, culminating in this end-times Movement of the Church of God. The result was an elevated self-understanding of the early Movement that rested heavily on the "prophetic" books of Daniel and Revelation.

This was a potent mix of perceptions that set the Movement's faithful on a crusade against the denominations in the name of holiness and unity. Time has shown that the call to renewed holiness of believers and their "churches" was sound. The judgment that a unified church is important for the effectiveness of its mission in the world was sound. The expectation of the soon return of Christ, however, was not, and the prophetic reading of church history that so enthused this Movement soon would prove as fragile as it was thrilling.

F. G. Smith's 1908 book *The Revelation Explained* gathered up the prophetic thoughts in the minds of pioneers Daniel S. Warner and W. G. Schell. At least until about 1935, it helped this prophetic pattern of Bible reading be widely assumed as critical biblical truth. It encouraged a separatism from the rest of the body of Christ, enabling the most "sectarian" phase of the Movement's life. The Church of God Movement stood over against all the "churches," while proclaiming God's intended unity of the church. The saints of the "Evening Light" understood themselves to be the restored church of the New Testament. All others were called to "come out" and join the Movement's final restoration crusade.

This originating vision needs to be understood if today's Church of God Movement is to reshape its self-understanding wisely for the sake of its own identity and future ministry. To understand the Movement of yesterday requires understanding the place, time, and thinking of its beginnings, and particularly the person who was its primary pioneer, Daniel S. Warner (1842-1895).[18] He is to be *remembered* and appreciated, but not *reverenced* and mimicked. He was a man of God and of his times.

Certain originating assumptions of the Movement would not stand the test of time. The launching holiness vision holds rich and enduring biblical support and spiritual validity. The longing for the church's renewed unity for the sake of its mission has not lost its relevance. The framework of biblical prophecy that came to surround these themes of holiness and unity, however, was borrowed, speculative, questionable, and would not withstand future scrutiny.

On the positive side, Warner's passion for holiness, true personal transformation by the redeeming power of Christ, is rightly seen as always belonging on the church's center stage. It's the one dynamic that can bring health to the church and unity among its members, regardless of human traditions, creeds, denominational labels, or biases that linger around gender and racial identities. Warner was once beaten nearly to death in Mississippi because he refused to discriminate against persons of color who came to his preaching sessions. Gifted women were gladly welcomed into the Movement's singing, teaching, and preaching ranks. These were early examples of an inclusive and liberating holiness still needed in today's church.

But there was a negative side of Warner's passion that was empowered in part by the specialized framework of biblical prophecy into which his holiness-unity passion soon found itself. The glowing spiritual dynamic became overlaid with a perspective that bred an arrogant and sometimes even nasty exclusivism. There was no room in God's flock, it was believed, for any sheep who refused to see and embrace the Movement's "evening light" on the church. This anti-sectarian Movement quickly hardened into the sectarian practice of dividing believers into those who would "come out" and those who choose to remain in the failed human frameworks of Christian church life.

For example, hear these harsh and divisive words. "There is in these last days a large sisterhood of Protestant bodies calling themselves churches, but the Lamb's wife owes no kin to them. They are of an entirely different family. Their mother is 'Mystery Babylon, the mother of harlots'."[19] The Roman Catholic Church was identified as the primary source of the evils that were corrupting Christianity, and her Protestant daughters were judged to be carrying the demonic disease. Coming out into the light of the Movement's grand vision, and presumably into the

Movement itself, was the only proper option for true believers willing to help prepare the church for the soon-returning Christ.

One of these supposed "harlot daughters" was the Free Methodist Church with which I have many family ties. I came to Christ in a Free Methodist camp meeting in East Liverpool, Ohio. Those were good Christian people who hung a huge banner behind the tabernacle pulpit that read "*HOLINESS UNTO THE LORD.*" How shocked I was much later to discover in the *Gospel Trumpet* publication of the Church of God Movement a field report of saints of the young Movement having "infiltrated" this very tabernacle of my conversion. These Movement representatives had stood uninvited at testimony time to announce boldly to the shocked crowd that they were freed of such Babylonian apostasy as the F-M Sect!

The report concluded that faces "grew very dark." Of course they would have! Holiness guests, supposedly advocates of Christ's uniting love, would hardly further their cause of uniting the ruptured Body of Christ in such a harsh and arrogant manner. One response was the Free Methodist Church soon referring in print to the Church of God Movement as the *NO-SECT-SECT.*[20] Unfortunately, too often representatives of the Movement acted that way, especially in its first generations.

Things had to and would change, but only slowly and painfully. The overlay of biblical prophecy encouraged arrogance and often brought destructive results. Before that changed, however, it would be deepened by the extremely popular writings of F. G. Smith, including his 1908 book *The Revelation Explained.* They solidified a self-understanding of the Movement that would be entrenched for decades.

These writings of Smith projected an exciting and dramatic picture. In exact fulfillment of biblical prophecy, God was said to have begun in A. D. 1880 to raise up a holy ministry to send forth God's Word against "sect-Babylon," calling his people out of centuries of compromise and apostasy. Through these called-out people, God was restoring the church as it was in the apostolic days. The "final reformation" was on!

It became widely believed that this glorious and predicted "coming out" was not a fanciful dream but the sure word of biblical prophecy, and thus it could not fail. This sureness eventually would change and bring into question some of the aspects of the original self-understanding of the Church of God Movement. Before the pain of that change, however, there was the power of a dramatic Movement identity.

NEEDED CONVERSATION AND ACTION

Without a vision the people perish. The early Church of God Movement surely had a powerful originating vision. It shaped the Movement's self-understanding and enabled it to launch its end-times mission and face boldly all persecution.

1. Do you understand this originating vision of the Movement, and see its motivational power? Are its *two phases* of the vision clear to you? They are:

    a. Realizing that there was a desperately needed *holiness renewal* of both individual believers and the church itself, a renewal that would enable a spiritual unity among all the sanctified on behalf of the church's redemptive mission in the world.

    b. Importing from others a particular way of reading *biblical prophecy*. This way clearly bolstered the exciting self-understanding of the new Movement as the concluding phase of all of church history.

2. Does this two-phased originating vision still exist in our time as a driving force for inspiring the Movement's self-understanding? Is it now defining the Movement's role in the Christian world? Are both phases still alive, or only one, or neither?

3. Is it possible that today the Movement has lost entirely a motivating vision? If so, can it long survive that way?

4. Who can/should do what to answer these questions? Is ignoring them a viable option for the Movement's future? What can you do to stimulate the needed conversation about establishing today's needed vision of the Movement's current identity?

5. As you interact with Christians not associated with the Church of God Movement, do you criticize them for not "seeing the light on the church"? Can you explain what that light is?

6. If you and many others don't see clearly the Movement's original vision, and wouldn't share it if you did, what's now holding the Church of God Movement together? Has some new vision taken over, or is there none at all?

CONTOURS of a CAUSE

The Theological Vision of the
Church of God Movement (Anderson)

Barry L. Callen

THIS · IS
THE WAY IT WAS

Growing Up in   the Church of God

ROBERT H. REARDON

Chapter 3

THE PAIN OF
A CHANGED IDENTITY

Much soon changed for the Church of God Movement. It was not surprising from a sociological point of view. Such "radical" reform groups usually grow rapidly in their early years. Why? "Because they provide dramatic answers to questions which deeply bother potential adherents." However, in most cases "it gives way to accommodation patterns, developing new institutional forms as the needs of the people change. Starting as a conflict group, the radical reform ultimately becomes an accommodating group."[21] God is unchanging, of course, but the church always has a human side.

Here, then, are key questions. Is accommodation inevitable? If it is, should accommodation to new circumstances to be viewed as necessary *adjustment* or unacceptable *compromise*? New circumstances do arise. Generations shift. The Bible stays the same, but readings of it change. The same Spirit keeps working, but that working becomes understood differently. As the winds of God blow in altered situations, do the followers of Christ flow with the Spirit or insist that what was once understood must always be understood in the same way? If a reform movement ever stops moving and adjusting, would it still be a movement?

The thrill of the launching vision of the Church of God Movement soon was tempered by several intruding realities. Christ failed to return as expected. The early support of the vision by a particular reading of biblical prophecy began to be questioned. Cultural shifts, new relationships, and necessary institutionalizing all appeared. A broader understanding of church history was gained and soon shifted the understanding of the Movement's place within it.

Such developments inevitably brought change. Again, was this change a weakening of the original vision or only a necessary and acceptable adjustment of it? Whatever the answer, a revised identity of the Movement had to be sought in the growing confusion and pain of the identity vacuum soon left by the changing of the Movement's original self-understanding. The simplicity, spontaneity, and power of offering dramatic answers to pressing questions in the 1880s tended to fade in the mix of emerging new realities in the 1920s and beyond.

Pioneers of the Movement had received "new light" on the church. Within a few generations, however, that light was dimmer and less commonly understood. Let's glance at how the original burst of idealism, bolstered by a given understanding of biblical prophecy, came to be experienced after half a century had passed.

The Light Dims

Beginning in 1899 and right into the 1920s, there was a series of disruptions in the life of the Church of God Movement itself. They were caused by groups that might be labeled "progressives" and "reactionaries." Some in Movement ranks questioned the implementation and even continuing validity of the original reformational vision. It had been one of moving dramatically to a pure, Spirit-filled, and Spirit-directed church. It was supposed to be the end-times church existing in sharp contrast to the jaded culture of the time and the human machinery of the established denominations. Were such negative things creeping into the Movement itself by the 1920s? Some said they were. Others justified them as absolutely necessary.

Robert H. Reardon reported on his boyhood in the Movement of the 1920s. He was "thoroughly Church of God." His father, Rev. E. A. Reardon, had been the first Chair of the General (Ministerial) Assembly of the Church of God when it formed in 1917. Here's the son's report of the Movement culture of his youth:

> I knew we were pilgrims in a strange land. The political world, higher
> education, the amusement world, the world of commerce and entertainment were not for us. We [the Church of God Movement] were God's
> people. We dwelt for only a brief time here in the world. Heaven was our
> home and our prayer was to make it. Marriage outside the church family

was strongly discouraged. I used to sing "the days of sex and creeds for us forevermore is past," *until I learned better.*[22]

The "sex" in the song lyrics, of course, was really "sects." Clarification is also needed for Reardon's key phrase that launched another stage in the pilgrimage of this Movement people. It's the "until I learned better."

Robert Reardon later would become an honored leader in American higher education beginning in the late 1950s. He had entered "other worlds" without leaving the changing world of the Church of God Movement. By then the whole Movement was having to do some hard rethinking about itself. President Reardon observed this to the Anderson College (University) Board of Trustees in 1979 on the eve of the Movement's centennial celebration: "Our historic antagonism to anything creedal in nature has left the Church of God drifting too much at the mercy of current winds of doctrine, and new people among us have had a hard time finding out who we are and what kind of theological cement holds us together." None formally did.

Some of the earlier cement clearly had eroded by the 1970s. And it wasn't just "new people" who were having difficulty understanding what the Movement was all about. Its constituency as a whole was then living in a world very different from that of the 1880s. Many Movement people were having increasing difficulty knowing exactly what the Movement believed or was called to be and do. Christ still had not returned and many other cultural and theological things were adding to the confusion.

The church is to be a special people called out of "the world" by God. But how cloistered should it be from the world around it, including isolation from other Christians who don't have "the light" on the church that the Movement's pioneers had seen? And what exactly is that light? The Movement had understood itself to be called to "come out" of the tainted church world and be truly different. But that difference, even in the name of reaching for true Christian holiness and unity, sometimes had morphed over the generations into a "holier than thou" separateness. Had it also compromised and become subtly captive to the dominant church and even secular cultures around it?

In preparing the biography of Lillie S. McCutcheon,[23] I discovered this from her childhood in Pennsylvania. The little Church of God congregation there, led mostly by her Sowers family that had been "brought out" of Lutheranism by Movement evangelists, became aware of a wonderful quartet from a nearby congregation in the Wesleyan-Holiness Christian tradition. The question was, "Can they come to our church and sing some Sunday?" The answer was clear. "No, because they haven't 'seen the light'." That meant they hadn't "come out" to the vision of the true church being enjoyed by the Movement. Even when seeking a renewed Christian unity, many of the Movement's representatives judged that some sharp lines of separation must be honored, even between Christians.

Soon that Sowers family, including young daughter Lillie, moved to northeastern Ohio, with the mother founding there a new congregation of the Movement in Newton Falls. My grandfather, Charles VanArsdale, a staunch Free Methodist by church tradition, took me there as a boy in the 1950s. He had found it to be the only church in the little town that was pastored by a strong biblical preacher, "Sister Lillie." He warned me, however, that she sometimes gave lectures on the Book of Revelation that were very questionable and narrowly sectarian. I should ignore them. I tried, although the big charts were very engaging.

I was totally unaware that by then some scholars of the Movement were agreeing with my uneducated grandfather. Sister Lillie had been ordained in 1947, with the hands of F. G. Smith on her shoulders. She sensed his mantle falling on her, encouraging her to continue his proclaiming of a particular reading of the Book of Revelation, the one so influential in earlier generations of the Movement.[2] She would do just that, even while by then the Movement at large was moving in the opposite direction.

The Pain of Significant Change

"The days of sects and creeds for us forevermore is past" was still a dominant belief in the 1930s and 1940s of Sister Lillie's childhood. These words were sung lustily in many settings of Movement life. Aspects of this slogan, however, already were being questioned. As early as 1920, H. M. Riggle, a close associate of pioneer leader Daniel Warner, had stopped teaching Warner's "church-historical" interpretation of the Book of Revelation, essentially the one later popularized by F. G. Smith and then Lillie S. McCutcheon. Riggle had come to believe that such an approach relies on the questionable assumption that the biblical symbols depict in advance the historical experiences of the church between the first and second comings of Christ.

Riggle had other concerns. He also was critiquing the impractical methods of the pioneer preachers who had been intensely opposed to any organization in church life (fearing the intrusion of more denominationalism). The "flying ministers" of the early Movement years had focused on the immediate and failed to equip converts to build for the long-term. That had been natural for them since they assumed the long-term wouldn't exist because of Christ's expected soon return. Many of the earliest Movement congregations had ceased to exist by the 1920s.[25] They had been founded largely by on-the-move ministers and not nurtured by settled and supported pastors. They had not been encouraged and equipped to maintain and build their corporate lives.

Various problems were painfully obvious by the 1920s. A big one, of course, was that Christ had not returned as expected two generations earlier. So, in this unexpected and awkward interim, Movement leaders faced the growing need to improvise, even modestly organize their mission and ministries together. The simplicity of the Movement's initial spontaneous existence was ending and its supposed innocence of the claimed apostasy of the outside denominational world was becoming less clear.

Early into the twentieth century, leaders of the Movement found themselves needing to set up a Missionary Committee, begin a little school, Anderson Bible Training School, and even establish in Anderson, Indiana, several ministry agencies, Christian Education, Church Extension, etc. These were being judged necessary to meet new needs and opportunities surfacing in the Movement's expanding life. Many leaders, however, were not sure of the appropriateness of these developments.

Establishing church institutions, of course, was being done reluctantly. No one wanted to become "just another denomination." Even so, ministry institutions began regardless of many ministers being uncomfortable in the presence of church "machinery" developing in response to pressing needs and opportunities, but without clear biblical warrant. Vigorous resistance to these developments caused the more "progressive" leaders to warn that blocking needed change only encouraged the accumulation of the smell of "sectarianism" on the clothes of the non-sectarian Movement.

E. A. Reardon was elected the first Chair of the Movement's General Ministerial Assembly in the United States and Canada, established formally in 1917. He addressed this central body in 1929, speaking frankly about a growing problem. "If this tendency to sectarianize ourselves is allowed to go to seed, it won't be long until we shall be numbered among the dead and be in the Babylonian Museum. Our people must not be so reformation centered as to be 'reformation sectarians,' making this reformation a fetish to be worshiped. There is no one body of people on earth who can claim an exclusive right to Christ and to all his light and truth."[26]

That was strong talk indeed. Reardon, as would be his son Robert after him, was courageous and colorful. E. A. went on to say this to the ministers in 1929. "I believe in a clear, separate, and distinct work for God, but I also believe that we should keep the sectarian stink out of the distinction." He promptly was voted out of his official roles, something hardly surprising. He accepted gracefully the negative vote and remained highly respected by many.

This strong anti-sectarian caution of Reardon's was announced at a time when the Movement was facing another problem not welcomed by many. The power of the Movement's original identity was beginning to weaken and being forced to shift. A major framework for supporting the early identity, the Movement's supposed being the fulfillment of biblical prophecy, was being brought into question.

A Prophetic Framework Falters

I grew up and was wonderfully nurtured by the Church of God congregation in Newton Falls, Ohio, and its outstanding pastors, the sister and brother team of Lillie McCutcheon and Austin Sowers. Sister Lillie was a modern-day lecturer on the Book of Revelation in the tradition of Warner, Schell, and F. G. Smith.[27] I recall in "home church" the graphic depictions of beasts and dragons hanging on the walls when lecture time came.

The drama of such biblical interpretation was impressive. Increasingly, however, this approach to "prophetic" biblical materials was becoming questionable across the Movement, especially in its institutions of higher education. The questioning that I soon experienced in my own education in the 1960s had begun for the whole Movement back in the 1920s and 1930s. It would only increase in the coming decades.

Thinking of the people who comprise the Movement today, relatively few are even aware of such lectures on biblical prophecy. The symbols in the Book of Revelation are not understood to have anything to do with why they are associated with the Movement. What happened to such a powerful undergirding portion of the originating vision of the Movement? Lillie McCutcheon was still representing it passionately into the 1990s, but only she and a very few others. How did something so prominent in the early generations of the Movement become discredited or at least widely ignored in later decades?

The answer in part is that key young leaders of the Movement went to prominent graduate schools. There they discovered other and apparently more responsible options for interpreting the Bible's "prophetic" materials, and thus a different understanding of church history and the Movement's role in it. In time, these new intellectual currents flowed into the Movement's own schools and encouraged a widespread abandonment of the earlier understandings. Replacing this loss with something of equal motivational power hasn't happened to date. This failure to replace a significant motivational loss is creating a widespread and paralyzing vacuum of vision in the Movement's life today.

Again, how did such a great loss happen? As the Great Depression was settling down on the United States and much of the world in 1929-30, a soul-wrenching struggle was raging in the Church of God Movement. Early blows included Russell R. Byrum and his teaching at the young Anderson school (Anderson University) across the street from the Gospel Trumpet Company in Anderson, Indiana. F. G. Smith was the highly influential Editor of the publishing company who saw himself called to be a leading shaper of Movement thinking. By contrast, Byrum was functioning more as an academic who identifies available options for students and does not push a particular view, including how best to interpret biblical books like Daniel and Revelation.

Word reached Smith that Byrum was presenting students with multiple interpreting approaches and failing to be clear that the Smith approach (as in his *The Revelation Explained*) was the correct one. As an educator and not indoctrinator, Byrum persisted in his anti-Smith approach. This led to a virtual "heresy" trial during the 1929 Camp Meeting in Anderson. Byrum was cleared of all charges, but felt himself tainted by the uproar. He chose to resign from the school's faculty rather than be an ongoing political problem for it. This was the loss of one of the finer minds the Movement had known, as seen in Byrum's authoring of the 1925 *Christian Theology* volume that was used for decades across the Movement despite the uproar.

The 1929 "trial" had fallout for more than Byrum. It revealed a deep tension already existing in the Movement. As viewed by the "progressives" of the time, Smith was turning his strong convictions about "the truth" into an effort at church-wide thought control approaching a renewed sectarianism. This was contrasting with the non-creedal stance of the Movement and had to be resisted.

Smith attempted to have the General Ministerial Assembly declare as authoritative "standard literature" of the Movement only material published prior to 1924, thus excluding Byrum's 1925 *Christian Theology.* While such a declaration would protect Smith's teaching on the Book of Revelation as the Movement's exclusive view, the majority of ministers resisted, judging such a declaration too much of a "creedal" slamming of the door to further truth, something the denominations routinely did. Smith felt that he was only protecting biblical truth and the Movement's integrity as he understood it.

Then in 1930 came a shock. Smith failed to be re-elected as Editor, a very influential position in the Movement's life. He was replaced by Charles E. Brown, a "progressive." Smith, wounded by being set-aside, assumed a prominent Ohio pastorate and completed his significant ministry in constructive ways, even helping to heal deep relational wounds in the Movement inflicted by others in the 1940s. Even so, a major shift had taken place in the Movement's thought life.

Beginning in 1930, Charles E. Brown would steadily guide the Movement in continued rethinking of many of its earlier assumptions. He would publish extensively, seeking to lift the Movement out of its general ignorance of church history. He would point to the Movement's role within the church's "radical" stream. Instead of it being a novel and dramatic spearhead of purifying the true church just before the return of Christ, it now was pictured as the latest in a series of similar reform movements over many centuries. Classic examples are Pietism, Moravianism, Methodism, and even some of the charismatic movements and Roman Catholic religious orders.

More troubling to some, while liberating to others, was the judgment that every stage of the development of the Church of God Movement "was comparable to the growth of other Protestant movements in church history."[28] Brown explained that the Movement's pioneers, largely unaware, had joined a long tradition of vigorous church reformers, some also using the Book of Revelation to understand themselves and their times.[29] Daniel Warner had contacted this tradition with his careful reading of Uriah Smith, Adventist scholar who used the Book of Revelation extensively in relation to his own reform movement.[30]

Now, by contrast, in the 1930s "the triumphalist voice of come-out-ism" was growing largely absent. For Brown, the Movement was less the goal of the divinely-directed historical process and more "the latest example of a radical Christianity that had been present all along the road from the Apostles forward."[31] The roots of Warner's thinking were unearthed. They included echoes of John Wesley, the large influence of John Winebrenner, Uriah Smith's whole prophetic scheme, etc. The Movement was not as unique and final as first believed, and not the direct and unique fulfillment of biblical prophecy. This realization was painful, welcomed by some but not at first accepted by many.

If Brown's new historical perspective was not enough to undercut the rationale for the Movement supposedly being found in biblical prophecy, the challenge of new biblical scholars in the Movement's life eventually would be. This is not to say that occasional interest in the original "prophetic prop" for the originating vision has ever disappeared. In the person of Lillie McCutcheon, for instance, it was still alive into the 1990s. But by then another prominent woman, Marie Strong of the Anderson University faculty, was vigorously countering such prophetic interest with her biblical scholarship.)[32] Since Marie Strong have come other scholars with similar concerns, including the current Timothy Dwyer of Warner University.[33]

Before Strong and Dwyer had been a series of others, especially Otto F. Linn and Adam W. Miller. Linn insisted that the Book of Revelation be read as the author intended and the original audience would have understood—encouragement for a persecuted church in the Roman Empire.[34] Major leaders of the Movement like Albert F. Gray and Gene W. Newberry began saying that the Movement's divine origin does not depend on any questionable interpretation of biblical prophecy but on the truthfulness and power of the New Testament's basic gospel message.

The newer approach of these biblical scholars was that "apocalypses" were written during times of persecution in order to encourage God's people. Good and evil come into conflict, but eventually the good will triumph. John and the early church faced such persecution, leading the Book of Revelation to picture the struggle and extend the hope. Since such conflict continues, the final book of the Bible remains very relevant, although the writer and readers of the first century were not "predicting"

in advance any particular set of future circumstances. Any such reading
of the biblical text is speculative at best, tends to be self-serving, and mis-
handles the Bible by reading back into the original what is not there.

What had become clear to many was that the Church of God Movement is a current example of the "charismatic" model of church renewal.
The church is seen "as essentially a spiritual organism. Institutional
forms are viewed ambivalently or totally rejected. In their concern for
present spiritual experience, they may fall prey to apocalyptic, dispen-
sational, or millennial views that are unbiblical and unrealistic."[35]Had
that happened to the Movement in its early years? Much evidence points
that way.

What is Adequate for Today?

The original vision of the Church of God Movement was about holiness
received and the resulting new potential of achieving real Christian
unity. Both holiness and unity are gifts of God to be activated by the
faithful for the good of the whole church. This vision was then bolstered
by a dramatic although now questioned reading of biblical prophecy.
Consequently, an important question arose and still lingers unanswered.
In the absence of any biblical prophecy as direct support for the Movement's existence, what's left? Whatever it is, can it stand on its own and
motivate future generations of the Movement to bring the significant
church reform needed?

These urgent questions became common by the 1920s. Relatively few
of those now in the Movement are even aware of the original thinking
about biblical prophecy's role in the Movement's self-understanding or
of the Movement's altered understanding of its presumed role in relation to the whole of Christianity. All of this shifting has been painful,
confusing, and it's ongoing, at least among the relatively few now concerned about such things. It's created a suffocating vacuum of Movement self-understanding.

The Movement's natural instinct across its generations has been "de-
constructionist," the hope of dismantling corrupt establishments in
church life, be they theologies, institutions, or practices. The dilemma
for the Movement has become this. Over time even a reform movement
develops its own institutions and "traditions of the elders." When this
is recognized, some change is needed. What kind remains a matter of
debate.

Times of change in the Movement's life often have been resisted by "conservatives." They have treasured the past and seen wisdom in its continuance relatively unchanged. Change is encouraged by the "progressives" who are more willing to alter the past in ways thought more appropriate and viable for the future. Such people don't necessarily call for new institutions, programs, or increased centralization of control, although often they have. What they always are ready to do is be open to rethinking the past and re-evaluating the Movement's present perspectives, relationships, and practices.

As the Movement's generations have come and gone, considerable change has happened. The conservatives have stood their ground and the progressives have spoken their mind and consistently made a difference. How to evaluate that difference is a matter of judgment. What is clear is that the time again has come for considering more change.

New Ideas and Attitudes

There have been several close calls that helped determine the future of the Church of God Movement. As noted above, E. A. Reardon was voted out after his strident 1929 address to the General Ministerial Assembly, but graciously stayed the course and stood for his concerns. Russell R. Byrum faded away rather than strike back after he had been put on trial, but his "open" views would prevail nonetheless. F. G. Smith returned to the pastorate after being voted out of the editorship in 1930, with his strong stance on biblical prophecy eventually fading. To his credit, his strong love for the church managed to rise above the pain of his rejected circumstance.

There also was the close call of John A. Morrison, the first president of Anderson College. He, like Russell Byrum, believed deeply in the value of education and was skillful in taking necessary steps to secure its future in the Movement. Morrison stood for ratification as president in 1934 and F. G. Smith and his loyal followers in Ohio and elsewhere were determined to have the General Ministerial Assembly change presidents and the "liberal" direction of the school.

Smith, then pastoring in Ohio, wanted the Anderson school to drop its new "liberal arts" curriculum and return to a simple Bible-school format. This "Ohio Uprising" of 1933-34 demanded that the school teach the Movement's "standard literature" and adhere to strict Church of God doctrine.[36] It was the clash between the freedom to entertain new thoughts and the urge to avoid change and protect the Movement's traditional identity and thinking.

The final vote on Morrison's ratification was close, but he survived, and so did the freedom of the Movement to keep thinking, growing, and moving ahead. Despite the deep divide in the Movement of that time, "the college's intellectual future, and in some measure the theological future of the Church of God Movement, would not be tied to a narrowly framed ecclesiology that a growing number of people considered outmoded."[37] Put otherwise, the anti-sectarian Movement would not be sectarianized. The "stink" would be kept out of its distinction.

Robert Reardon, Morrison's eventual successor as president Anderson College (University), recalled this about the dilemmas always faced by the president of a Christian college. Dr. Morrison's formula for institutional success, Reardon reported, had been "to convince the church we were spiritual, to convince the accrediting organizations we had brains, and to show the sports world we were winners." He added from his own experience that "dealing with the General Assembly of the Movement is like entering the pool at Bethesda, only in reverse. You never want to go in when the waters are troubled!"[38]

The Movement's early "come-outism" stance, supposedly supported by biblical prophecy, was still deeply entrenched in the Movement of the 1920s and 1930s, but it was steadily weakening. Otto F. Linn was the first to earn an academic doctorate in the Movement. He used his new knowledge to bolster the innovative work of Charles E. Brown and the growing sense of the Movement needing to discard its old framework of biblical prophecy. I would follow Linn's lead when preaching on the occasion of the 100th anniversary of the Movement in Jamaica. I was asked to preach in Kingston on the Book of Revelation since it was so significant in the Movement's history.

I said to that celebrating West Indies crowd that the last book of the New Testament has only two main points. To the church of ancient Asia under great pressure, the first point is that Jesus is *Lord of the church*, not the powerful of this world! To the church of any time and place, the second point is that Jesus is *Lord of all history and of all that will follow the ending of this world!* The final New Testament book completes the needed bookends for the whole Bible. Genesis declares that *in the beginning*, God, and Revelation declares that *in the end*, God!

Multiple Shifts Experienced

The issue of biblical prophecy is emphasized here because of its particular importance in the changing self-understanding of the Church of God Movement. But there were other things, many others that also have been agents of change. Some have been the passing of prominent people. In the absence of established and authoritative church institutions, "charismatic" leaders have been particularly beloved and influential in the Movement's life.

For example, shocking news came just before Christmas, 1895. Daniel Warner was dead! There were grieving saints far and wide, with Warner's remains viewed by a large and weeping crowd in Grand Junction, Michigan. For the young Church of God Movement, this was the end of the beginning. What would come next was unknown. Could the Movement go on without this visionary pioneer? Yes, it would go on in the hearts and with the hands of others, but it wouldn't ever be quite the same. Movements over time never are.

What would come after was fresh biblical interpretation and institutional growth that could not have been foreseen by the Movement's primary pioneer. Significant cultural shifts began to happen after his death. By the 1950s the Movement was slipping "across the tracks" and into the mainstream of American Protestantism. Those post-war years saw a growing attendance and prosperity in most religious communities, including the Church of God Movement. There was a boom in church building, with architectural designs featuring beauty as well as function. This suggested that the constituency of the Movement was joining the middle class in the United States, and with this joining was coming an elevated image consciousness.

The Movement, against its own will, was moving subtly from being a protest group to more of an established church body.[39] The Movement now existed in numerous countries outside North America with their differing cultural circumstances and approaches to church organization and life in general.

Definitions of "holiness" were also shifting, and the prominence of this doctrine in the Movement's preaching was fading. Two major Church of God hymnals appeared in 1953 and 1971. They included fewer hymns and gospel songs by Movement composers and carried fewer traditional Movement emphases. There was an increased presence of songs popular in American Protestantism generally.

Meanwhile, two worldwide shifts in Christianity had appeared, each featuring one of the central concerns of the Movement. Ironically, these appearings were mostly without the Movement's participation and usually proceeded in the face of its criticism. They were the "charismatic" movement (stressing a holy and gifted life in the Spirit) and the "ecumenical" movement (stressing that church unity must be made more evident for the sake of the church's world mission).

The twin concerns of the Movement, the needed holiness and unity of God's people, were becoming central in the Christian world of the 1960s-1980s, but not exactly as the Movement had conceived and taught them. Where did this leave the Movement? Generally on the outside of things given the Movement's stances of not being "joiners" but being active criticizers of the perceived wrongs of others. It left the Movement without much witness beyond its own small constituency. The Movement had quietly joined the mainstream of Protestantism and yet stood aloof from it, and for the most part and had little influence on it.

Significant shifts in American culture had clearly affected the Movement. In the first years of the twentieth century, the shift was seen particularly in the liberalizing of dress and dietary standards. A major "Necktie Controversy" flared for a time in the Movement. Christian men (mostly rural in background) who chose to wear neckties were viewed as joining a self-centered fad of secular and urban men. Many other points of tension came along until, by the 1960s, the Movement "could no longer be described as a sectarian protest Movement."[40] In the first decades of the twenty-first century, the continuing shifting now includes an ever-widening range of issues.[41]

How should the Movement now view and react to all this change? Not necessarily with alarm. What must not happen is denial of the shifting realities or any abortive attempt to mimic the Movement's beginnings while living in dramatically different circumstances. The Movement initially was a classic example of a "sect" reality, one that ironically was vigorously "anti-sectarian." Change came rather quickly. This happens in the natural course of things to nearly all protest groups in the church.

A "sect" is a radical renewal movement that initially is very negative to the existing churches which are viewed as seriously compromised. The renewal movement severely judges, isolates itself from the negative morass, and is determined to spearhead a recovery crusade appointed by God. That clearly was the Church of God Movement in its earliest generations.

In the 1880s there had been serious wrongs in church life. It is understandable that this would cause sincere Christians to "come out," determined to pay whatever price necessary to address the problems head-on. As a sociologist from within the Movement has explained: "This is the everlasting process of reviving the church. The sects are safety valves, letting off the steam of over-institutionalization, of clumsy ecclesiastical machinery that runs simply for the sake of running."[42] Then comes the sect's own accommodations, adjustments, its more balanced view of the "outsiders." There comes a growing awareness that the renewal movement itself has "matured" institutionally and is not above criticism itself.

How a reform movement handles these typical changes is very important for its future. It's appropriate to be proud of the Movement's renewal heritage and its dramatic attempts to correct wayward church life. Once having advanced beyond its own "sect" origins, however, a renewal body like this Movement is faced with a vacuum in its own life. It isn't all that it once was. It's now very sensitive about the danger of becoming what it always has criticized. It must envision fresh and constructive beginnings for itself in a new time.

In this vacuum, this awkward stage of its own development as a formalized body, the Movement has begun quietly to look for some clarity about its ongoing identity and mission. It needs a new self-understanding and reason for being in these very new times, and in this new stage of its own development. This needed fresh envisioning is as difficult to accomplish as it is necessary to attempt. Recognizing the need is an important first step.

In the next chapter we will review the life of the Movement in this extended and awkward vacuum of unclear identity and mission. That will set the stage for attempting in the final chapters to explore themes and actions that appear appropriate and crucial for the Movement's future in these very new times.

NEEDED CONVERSATION AND ACTION

Without a vision the people perish. The Church of God Movement certainly had a vision (chapter two) and then also has experienced a significant loss of portions of that vision (this chapter). Now what?

1. Surely a "movement" can find a way to move past the grief of a significant identity loss and open itself to some responsible replacement. But it's not easy. Is the Church of God Movement grieving the loss of much of its past and hanging on instead of moving on?

2. If a movement is really of God, is it necessarily susceptible over time to the usual sociological trends of other "organizations"? Is the church as we know it always a combination of the "human" and the "divine"? The Church of God Movement always has wanted the divine dimension of church life to dominate.

3. Some young scholars in the Movement completed advanced academic studies by analyzing the Movement, bringing new information and insights to its identity and mission. Were the Movement leaders who worried about the role of higher education correct or has it's schools been a great asset? A full history of higher education in the Church of God Movement is found in the book Enriching Mind and Spirit (see the Bibliography).

4. Repeatedly in major Movement self-studies, and as recently as "Project Imagine" (2017-18), insightful voices in the Movement have raised a core concern. They have said that the Movement must rediscover a compelling identity, not just tinker with its disjointed organizational machinery. We structure to implement who we are and what we are called to do. But who is the Movement now?

5. Is there still some "stink" in the Movement's "distinction"? Is the Movement still defining itself over against others? Who can and will frame a new vision for the Movement, one that fits today and does not violate the integrity of Scripture?

6. Is the Movement's role to proclaim and live out the title of Daniel Warner's biography, *It's God's Church!* ? Is it adequate to be assured that Jesus is the Subject, the Lord of the church, and the Lord of all history? Isn't that news exciting enough to propel the Movement forward today? On the other hand, isn't the lordship of Jesus what all Christians affirm? Does the Movement need some additional and distinctive self-understanding?

7. The church necessarily interacts with the culture of its surrounding society. Has the Movement interacted appropriately or compromised wrongly with the values and standards of today's society? Reading the next chapter should help with this question.

I Saw the Church

the life of the Church of God told theologically

by

Merle D. Strege

Chapter 4

THE PARADOXES OF LIFE IN A VACUUM

Is the Church of God Movement now without a rudder, quietly grieving the loss of what once was while moving wherever the contemporary winds blow, adjusting as necessary? There has been considerable interaction with "outside" forces over the decades and many resulting changes. The related paradoxes haven't been easy to live with and refuse to go away.

The year 2020 in the Western world is similar to recent decades of the life of the Church of God Movement. They are, in fact, disturbingly alike in some ways. Today there's much to celebrate and also so such rapid change that it's hard to be clear about basic things that used to be taken for granted. The result is destabilizing and worrisome.

Technological advances have been stunning, marvelous, and troublesome. The young now have their own worlds of electronic devices, gaming, and constant communication. The older generation feels left behind, with many of their fundamental assumptions questioned and their traditional jobs no longer needed or sent to other countries. Normal patterns of weather are being upset, bringing cries for dramatic defensive action, and also denials that it's even happening.

In the United States, there are calls to "Make America Great Again," with no consensus about what that means or how it should be done. While there is growing need to discover constants that can be relied on, there also is little consensus about what is really basic and would even work. Being "spiritual" has gained wide public interest, along with a wide range of definitions and practices.

Is the Church of God Movement really a "movement" anymore? Today's constituency doesn't agree on a definition or a direction in this regard. Many in its congregations aren't even conscious of being part of any "movement." They participate in whatever congregation meets their felt needs and preferred worship styles. This circumstance could be described as life in a vacuum for a Movement dedicated to dramatic church reform.

A Harsh Vacuum

All of this change and its resulting dilemmas are reflected in the Church of God Movement as it tries to function in today's very different social and religious world. The Movement has passed through a series of its own changes and often has tried to reach back for certainty about its own identity and mission. These reaching attempts have brought periods of disruption but no fresh consensus of self-understanding. Recent generations of the Movement have been living in an awkward vacuum, still alive but with difficulty breathing and growing. Yesterday is largely gone, while today is a mixed and confusing bag of new and stressful things.

The Movement has been held together in recent years mostly by a network of personal relationships involving many wonderful people now residing in many nations. Most of the best known and respected leaders who have preserved the Movement's vision of itself now have died and taken with them much of the previous understanding of and loyalty to this reform tradition.

The organizational structures of today's Movement are fragmented and often distrusted, and they are supported only voluntarily by the congregations (see chapter ten). This provides the Movement with little "group glue" or dependable resources for cooperative ministries. The powerful originating vision of the Movement has been quietly abandoned in significant part by many of the Movement's own leading thinkers, and nothing of equal motivating power has yet emerged to replace it. The resulting vacuum is real and disabling.

Not far into the twentieth century, as noted above, leading Christian voices unrelated to the Movement began echoing the central concerns of the Movement— the vital need for real life in the Spirit to ensure the integrity of personal and church life (holiness) and the urgent need of Christian unity for the sake of the Christian mission (unity). The cries of Movement pioneers were beginning to be heard widely in the world church, but from mouths other than those of the Movement which chose to remain on the sidelines of these "ecumenical" and "charismatic" movements.

After the first few generations of the Movement's existence, various "traditions" of the Movement had solidified. That made it harder to keep claiming that the Movement still is a spontaneous dynamic of God so different from the settled and staid "denominations." Movement leaders increasingly have found themselves explaining that the Movement itself isn't the ideal it's been proclaiming. They also have been insisting that the Movement still doesn't want to become what most others assume it already is—another denomination. Progress may be in the right direction, but it's painfully slow and so much is pulling in wrong directions.

The Movement is caught between the ideal and the real. It's still proclaiming the whole family of God as the true church, while only a select few of all believers are coming to the Movement's family reunions. Most of the Movement's faithful were once reluctant to be involved with Christians who hadn't "seen the light." Now reunions of the Movement's faithful can't explain exactly what that "light" is.

For these and other reasons, the Movement has been living in an awkward vacuum since at least the 1950s. This awkward space, while empty of clarity, has been full of painful paradoxes. One is that this reform movement on behalf of Christian unity has been making few churchwide friendships outside the Movement. While a non-creedal body, the Movement has been most uncomfortable associating in formal and public ways with Christian bodies that believe in ways that differ from what has been standard in the Movement—even though "standard" belief is hardly a Movement ideal and is nowhere formally stated (see chapters 6 and 7).

The 1940s were terrible war years for the world and especially painful for the Movement. It was relatively isolated from the broader Christian community and also dealing with delicate and controversial transitions in its own life. It was questioning pioneer foundations in very different and volatile times. The "Watchmen on the Wall" struggle in the 1940s, for instance, was over the pride of the original Movement's identity seeming to be slipping away (see more on this below). The Movement was having to rethink itself while implementing new programmatic initiatives that looked much too "denominational" to particularly conservative pastors.

The continuing tensions in the Movement's life led to a key judgment on the eve of the Movement's centennial celebration in 1980. Three challenging paradoxes were then very evident. They were: (1) finding comfort when focusing on a vision of the pure church governed by God's Spirit while living with the practicalities of its humanly organized life; (2) finding ways of conceiving and achieving Christian unity in new and highly dynamic religious settings; and (3) recovering for the Movement a motivating sense of its identity and reason for continuing to be.[44]

Now, four decades after that centennial celebration, the Movement still appears to be struggling with essentially the same issues, having made little progress. Maybe, hopefully, recalling how the Movement has struggled in the past can encourage a new generation to find fresh answers for the future.

Air Hard To Breath

Living in a vacuum that lacks clear identity and direction is like gasping for life-giving air. Here are words from a young minister who helped spark the struggle of the Church of God Movement in the mid-twentieth century. They were spoken by the son of E. A. Reardon who had warned of the coming struggle back in 1929 (see above).

Robert H. Reardon announced this just before the Movement's centennial celebration in 1980. "With the collapse of 'last reformationism,' we seem lost on the scene without distinctives, without identity, and without comrades in arms. We have built few friendly ties with other Christian groups and have thrashed and alienated them."[45]

A key characteristic of the resulting vacuum and struggle has been *fear*. Here are some of the lingering fears that have been plaguing the Movement in recent generations.

1. Violating our own reform heritage by being involved with cooperative ministry efforts that may be less than the ideal in design or result. To do it right, must we do it ourselves? Dare we try doing it with others? Are only partial steps nonetheless acceptable steps?

2. Linking arms in ministry action with brothers and sisters in the faith who haven't "seen the light" as clearly as we. Can we tolerate the com-

promised witness that comes from questionable associations with denominational and ecumenical brothers and sisters?

3. Becoming "just another denomination" by actively strategizing and organizing for Christian mission. Isn't the likely result that soon we will be strangled by our own church machinery?

4. Finding new insights in the Bible that may put Movement pioneers in a bad light. Didn't this Movement have most things right from its beginning?

5. Affirming the great theological insights of church history. Isn't openly affirming any "creed" an unacceptable block to fresh thinking? On the other hand, doesn't fresh theological thinking run the risk of further threatening our Movement's precious heritage?

The Movement has lived with such fears for generations. They reached a high pitch of controversy in the 1940s and have not gone away.

Two early flashpoints were the 1943 master's thesis of Robert H. Reardon done at Oberlin Graduate School of Theology, and a reacting article in the *Gospel Trumpet* by L. Earl Slacum in September, 1944. The study focused on the changing doctrine of the church and Christian life in the Movement, and the article asked the provocative question, "Is An Apostasy Emerging?" The "Watchmen on the Wall" controversy flared and would upset the Movement across North America for several years. It was the clashing of key leaders, some concerned with changes threatening to compromise the past and others anxious to move ahead with long-needed change and new ministry structuring and programming.

One respondent to a survey used in the Reardon study summarized well the core tension in the Movement of the 1940s. "We have grown away from the 'special people' consciousness to a more universal Christian attitude. Without surrendering loyalty to truth, we have come to respect the beliefs of others. As ministers, we are willing to see our beliefs tried and tested and, if they are found wanting, to admit that they are wrong." Another respondent was more graphic while expressing a similar attitude: "We are getting out of the little theological ditch which we were supposed to walk in and ask no questions."

Such judgments caused Rev. Slacum to shift the traditional practice of "thrashing Babylon" (Movement outsiders) to attacking wayward leaders inside the Movement. After several years, the resulting turmoil quieted, a few small adjustments were made in the national offices, and Editor Charles E. Brown tried to put it all in historic perspective. He and others quietly worked to free new generations of the Movement from enslavement to its quite restrictive and ingrown past.

Even so, this struggle was not really over, and still isn't. It continues to twist about in a vacuum that lacks clear Movement identity. In such an awkward place, surrounded by competing cultures of secular and church life, adaptations (compromises?) are made and judged variously. Note this that was shared with the General Assembly in 2019:

> For too long we've groveled at the altar of a church growth phi-losophy that has been hijacked by some to mean that our mission is to make sure we offend no one by what and how we preach, teach, and live. The Church of God has a message today's church needs to hear, but we're too afraid of being unpopular to share it. Our Movement will not be what God has called it to be if we don't get ahead of the culture with the message God has given us. We have confessing and repenting to do on the subjects of women in ministry, racial unity, and cultural accommodation. Early in the Movement's history, we were ahead of the curve on all of these. In more recent years, however, we've quietly yielded to alien cultural pressures.[46]

Beginning in the 1950s, Philip Kinley served with his wife Phyllis for decades as Movement missionaries in Japan. They represented well the Christian faith in a nation with very few Christians. Phil eventually was honored by the Emperor for his outstanding educational service to the children of that nation. Looking toward home from the Far East, Phil observed that "one of the big problems facing the Church of God Move-ment in America is how to be relevant to its culture without becoming its prisoner." Yielding to alien cultures is a real danger, especially for a church reform movement valuing local independence that frees each congregation to do as it sees best in its particular setting and surround-ing influences.

Kinley pointed to America's success-oriented culture that encourages the church to assume that every year it should produce bigger budgets, better programs, and winning numbers of converts and church plantings. Enough money and effort presumably will solve almost any problem, and if it's good enough for the United States it surely should be the standard for the world. He concluded: "Perhaps if we were humble enough to sit and learn at the feet of leaders from overseas, we would be delivered from a culture that threatens to imprison us."[47]

Had the American culture, and those of other church bodies, imprisoned the Church of God Movement with thinking and practices actually alien to the Movement? There certainly were tension points that suggested so. It's been and remains air difficult to breathe.

Particular Points of Tension

Seven particular areas of tension are clear examples of recent change in the life of the Church of God Movement. They've all involved the Movement's interaction with "outside" cultures and pressures. Each tension area has been encountered and accommodated in some way, sometimes negatively. All interactions have stressed and stretched the Movement. Some have led to important successes and some to unfortunate reverses.

1. Struggling with Racial Diversity. The Church of God Movement was welcoming of African-Americans from its beginning, some becoming outstanding leaders. In fact, the unusual fact that the Movement's constituency in recent decades has been nearly twenty percent African-American in the United States is the envy of other essentially "white" church bodies.

That said, the 1968 General Assembly still found it necessary to declare the area of racial inclusion a spiritual priority requiring attention. Considerable progress had been made in racial relations within the Movement, but more was needed. The Assembly resolved that the national boards and agencies of the church "be directed to make deliberate moves to secure Negro leaders for executive and/or administrative roles wherever and whenever possible, this being a way to show a more truly inclusive pattern for ourselves on the national level."

Ironically, while many outside the Movement have applauded its comparatively successful history of racial inclusiveness, the Movement has been aware of its incompleteness in this regard. The General Assembly called for repentance because of Movement failures. Numerous Assembly resolutions have focused on this subject over the years.[48] Cultural patterns and prejudices have infiltrated and sometimes controlled life in the Movement despite its enviable racial position in general.

The segregation of the races into separate congregations became a typical pattern in the Movement especially after World War I. Before that awful war there are reports that an awkward event had taken place at the Movement's central Camp Meeting in Anderson, Indiana. Apparently some city leaders met with church leaders to express concern about the large number of "colored" people descending on the city for Camp Meeting each summer. Reportedly (no written record), these church leaders then gathered some African-American brothers and sisters on the church grounds and suggested that, while they were most welcome, it might be best if they not come in such large numbers in the future. Theological idealism and prevailing social prejudice were coming into conflict.

The full story of race relations in the Movement has been well told by James Earl Massey.[49] While major leaders and preachers of the Movement have included outstanding African-Americans, unfortunately the traditional religious idealism and racial inclusion of the Movement has become infected to some degree by the problems of the United States and its history of racial discrimination. The Movement has struggled to remain a shining light amid surrounding darkness.

The National Association of the Church of God Movement, a large African-American organization, recently celebrated its centennial. I published an article highlighting this unique history and celebration.[50] The Christian ideal has struggled against the discriminatory racial history of the United States. The Movement has been both a gleaming light for others to follow and at times a light dimmed by external intrusions unredeemed by the liberating gospel of Christ. The Movement has reason to rejoice, and also to repent.

2. Affirming the Equality of Women in Church Leadership. Honoring diversity has been affirmed as a vital part of the very theological and social DNA of the Church of God Movement. It has affirmed a gift-based rather than gender-based leadership. "Forty years before the time of woman's suffrage on a national level [U.S.A.], a great company of women were preaching, singing, writing, and helping to determine the policies of the Church of God Movement."[51] Beginning in the 1930s,

Church of God women organized on a national scale and became substantial supporters of church mission at home and abroad.

Meanwhile, cultural pressure again began to intrude. It tended quietly to undermine the classic stance of the Movement that affirms the full equality of women in church ministry at all levels. The years between 1925 and 1975 were quite negative in regard to women functioning as pastors in the Movement. The percentage of congregations pastored by women dropped dramatically from 32% to 3%. "As the reform Movement developed institutional structures, doors once wide open to women closed almost completely."[52]

I grew up under the exceptional pastoral ministry of Rev. Lillie S. McCutcheon, but such female leadership had become uncommon. Countering the negative trend, she announced this to the Movement in 1989: "God is an Equal Opportunity Employer. One standard is set for both female and male Christians. All are saved the same way, entering through Christ. Requirements for baptism, sanctification, communion, and foot washing are alike for everyone. Paul expresses it well, 'There is neither Jew nor Greek, there is neither bond nor free, there is neither male nor female, for ye are all one in Christ Jesus' (Gal. 3:28). Preaching with authority is demanded by God, but the authority is in the Word—not in the preacher—be that preacher male or female."[53]

This trend against women in church leadership has been encouraged by many "evangelical" Christian leaders who rely on supposed New Testament teaching against women clergy. A female scholar of the Movement published a persuasive argument to the contrary.[54] Despite this major study, the prejudice has continued, often unspoken but significant and hurtful nonetheless.

A troubling question is whether the Movement has accommodated to prevailing standards of "evangelical" Protestantism that often does not accept women as equals in church leadership. A current leader in the Movement reports privately to me his feelings when he recently left a pastorate of the Movement to assume another position. "I was shocked at the response from a few Church of God lifers to the calling of a female pastor." Has the Movement accepted, at least in common practice, certain biblical interpretations alien to the Movement's own tradition?

Jeannette Flynn, a prominent national official of the Movement, suffered personally from a Church of God congregation infiltrated by Christian elements opposed to women in ministry. She and many others were surprised and dismayed when her pastoral candidacy was suddenly refused because she was female. On the other hand, two recent Chairs of the Movement's General Assembly in the United States and Canada have been female, evidence of the Movement defying a strong pulling the other way. It's been difficult to resist cultural pressures and supposed exclusionary biblical teaching.

3. Gaining Educational Respectability. From the founding of Anderson Bible Training School (Anderson University) in 1917, the Church of God Movement has had concern about formal training of the mind being in possible conflict with the spiritual gifting of the Spirit for ministry.[55] In 1946 the Anderson campus gained full regional accreditation. It had matured into a respectable academic institution recognized as having a quality liberal arts curriculum, acceptable academic standards, and a faculty educated in some of the finest institutions in the nation. Pacific Bible College (Warner Pacific University) was going through a similar process. Mid-America Christian University and Warner University soon would do the same.

This clash of cultures, the educational and church worlds, occasionally would surface in conflict. One key figure was Dr. Otto F. Linn who would teach prominently in two of the Movement's universities. Another was Dr. Robert H. Reardon, president of Anderson College (University) from 1958 to 1983. His biography is titled *Staying on Course*, pointing to his determination that both academic and church integrity can and should be present in the same institution. Defining academic integrity in a Christian setting, however, wouldn't be easy or always respected by a segment of the Movement's ministers.

Anderson University launched a seminary in the early 1950s with little awareness or support from the Movement at large. That School of Theology was struggling in the early 1970s when its president, Robert Reardon, linked it with an ecumenical, multi-seminary venture in nearby Indianapolis called the "Foundation for Religious Studies." Particularly because this collective included a small Roman Catholic seminary, controversy erupted in the Movement, forcing a quick end to this new relationship.

In the turmoil, the Anderson seminary gained attention and some new financial support through the General Assembly. Even so, graduate education for ministerial preparation was not and still is not required for ministerial ordination. Lacking larger relationships, the Anderson seminary today continues to struggle for a meaningful existence. Nonetheless, its faculty and graduates have had significant influence in the Movement's life ever since the 1950s.

The Church of God Movement came into being critiquing the evils of institutionalism in church life. Denominational institutions of higher education were special targets of criticism since they demanded considerable resources to perpetuate and often were used to extend to new generations the divisiveness of denominational loyalty. The Movement, however, soon found itself spawning its own schools, a few of which have grown and survived. Those now closed or merged into another institution include Arlington College, Bay Ridge Christian College, Gardner College, and Jamaica School of Theology. None of these were established by formal action of the Movement as a whole, but by the vision and determination of individuals or small groups who often acted in despite resistance from the larger body.[56]

The schools now surviving in the United States, four universities, are fully accredited by the appropriate educational agencies. A large portion of their students now come from other than congregations of the Movement and are not intending ministries within the Movement's life. Relatively few of these students arrive on campus motivated to focus their studies on the Bible, church history, Christian theology, or ministerial preparation. Instead, they are preoccupied with preparing for successful and well-paying careers in numerous fields not directly church-related—an obvious reflection of the prevailing culture and times.

Ironically, an early Movement critique of higher education focused on the supposed preoccupation of such institutions with indoctrinating students as a way of maintaining their sponsoring denominations. Such an accusation could hardly be leveled at the present institutions of the Movement, although they probably wish it were truer than it is.

4. Dealing with the Economic Marketplace. The Gospel Trumpet Publishing Company was the original organized ministry of the Church of God Movement. Its periodical, the *Gospel Trumpet* (later called *Vital Christianity*), was a major tool in the initial growth and ongoing cohesion of the Movement. Later known as Warner Press, this company became one of the larger religious publishers in the United States. It inevitably came to face the pressures of the economic marketplace outside the church.

The title of the company's published history, *Miracle of Survival*,[57] suggests the difficulty. It developed a separate division for its large non-church printing activities, struggled with employees moving to unionize, eventually ended its large printing operation and even had to end publishing its church periodical in 1996 because of lessening of "denominational loyalty" among constituents of the Movement.

Similar dynamics, including a particularly painful ending, were experienced by the church's Board of Church Extension and Home Missions. Beginning in the 1920s, this ministry served local congregations of the Movement in their facility and financial needs. But it also expanded into the larger marketplace of investments and came to suffer from a range of related issues. Legal challenges to this range and manner of operation came to involve costly legal action against it that stretched over years. Finally, early into the twenty-first century, the legal process led to the full dissolution of this ministry as a corporation. This was one of the more difficult and costly episodes ever faced by the Movement.

Another financial crisis resulted from the move of the campus of Mid-America Christian University from Houston, Texas, to Oklahoma City, followed by a long delay in selling the old property. National Movement intervention was required to save this school. The purpose of recalling this and the other crises is to point out that the Movement had entered worlds beyond the church and sometimes suffered accordingly. It's not that such moves should not have been made, but that the Movement was poorly equipped to face them well.

The church always struggles to be *in* but not *of* the world. Its institutional life, as feared from the Movement's beginning, tends to take on a life of its own, and necessarily interacts with the broader world and its contrasting values. Isolation is hardly the answer. Caution, however, is essential. There is danger involved in any more institutionalized pattern church life (see chapter ten).

5. Pondering Peace. If Jesus is the focus of the Christian faith and the Prince of Peace, what should be the stance of his disciples in the turmoil of world politics and persistent warfare? In the time of Jesus, his people longed for freedom from Roman occupation and hoped that their coming Messiah would lead the way in getting it done. Jesus came, however, as a "suffering servant" Messiah who didn't fulfill their expectation with a sword. He was rejected and executed at the urging of his own people.

The Church of God Movement has not been known as one of the classic "peace" churches (like the Quakers, Mennonites, etc.). Even so, throughout its history it has had a group of people within its ranks who have been highly sensitive to the irony of Christians being willing to support and actively participate in the brutality of warfare. They have been unwilling to risk compromising primary allegiance to God's kingdom by elevating "patriotism" to prominence. Russell Olt, Maurice and Dondeena Caldwell, Kenneth and Arlene Hall, John Albright, Hollis Pistole, Siegfried Pudel, and Fred and Kay Shively have been particularly prominent. They and others have comprised a relatively small but persistent "Peace Fellowship" of the Church of God, with the Caldwells enabling a peace program on the Anderson University campus.

The General Assembly of the Movement in the United States and Canada on occasion has addressed the subject of war.[58] It has seen it as highly undesirable, even anti-Christian, while also being supportive of its own young people who choose active military service. A prominent symbol of this dual stance is the presence on the campus of Anderson University of two neighboring buildings. One was originally dedicated by highlighting a Secretary of Defense of the United States and the other honoring a leading peace advocate of the Church of God Movement (Wilson Library and Olt Student Center).

Of particular concern is the observation that public stances of the Movement on the war-peace issue have seemed to adjust to the dominant political sentiments of the United States that shift in various times of peace and war. The Movement has appeared vulnerable to the political winds that surround it. One constant must be primary allegiance to the kingdom of God, which sometimes is in direct tension with any national "patriotism."

6. Authorizing a Clergy *Credentials Manual*. It wasn't until the 1940s that the General Assembly of the Movement in the United States and Canada first called for the development of a credentials manual to standardize the several and sometimes conflicting policies and processes of ministerial credentialing. The first manual didn't appear until the 1980s, and the first edition to be declared mandatory for use by all assemblies came only in 2017. By then ministers and congregations of all church bodies were increasingly under threat of legal action in relation to various standards of the culture. They needed to have in place clear guidelines closely tied to their religious beliefs and church affiliation if they were to function with integrity and legal safety.

The North American assemblies authorized to do credentialing in the Movement agreed to adopt and use the common manual exclusively, but some did so reluctantly. It took two years for all assemblies in the United States to agree formally, with one of the Canadian assemblies still uncommitted in 2020. Some struggled with the idea of institutionalizing credentialing in a mandatory system, something threatening to lessen the "autonomy" of the church at the local and area assembly levels. Was this a move toward obvious and unwelcome denominationalism?

Here was an instance when there was need to act in a way unusual for the Movement because of the threats of the surrounding social and legal environments. Viewing it more positively, it was the Movement finally acting intentionally and together for increased unity. Thinking negatively, it was increased institutionalizing forced from the outside and violating key values of the Movement.

7. Mistrusting "Liberal" Leadership. All generations of the Church of God Movement have been blessed with gifted and dedicated leaders. They sometimes wished to move forward in ways not comfortable to many "conservative" ministers. Especially beginning in 1917, with the launching of Anderson Bible Training School and then a series of national ministry organizations, deep tensions emerged in the Movement's life. While details vary, there have been several controversies that have brought considerable disruption to the Movement. They all have had the common concern about leaders thought to be crossing lines that should never be crossed. The ministry organizations and programs they were sponsoring appeared to some to be threatening the original genius of the Movement and the full control of the Spirit of God in the church.

Voices often call for a vision that can freshly define and motivate the Movement. But attempts to rally people behind such a vision are typically met with mistrust and resistance. It's difficult for leaders to move forward in a setting where there is an absence of any real authority. Beloved pastors such as Arlo Newell are brought to prominent national positions of leadership and sometimes then subjected to criticism when they take any real initiative. Such happened to Dr. Newell, he said, "merely because I changed my address to Anderson, Indiana." The leaders at "headquarters" (a word resisted vigorously) are the natural targets even of those who voted to have them there.[59] The current General Director refers to the Anderson church offices as "Basecamp."

The 2017 General Assembly of the Movement in the United States and Canada convened a century after its founding in 1917. It took two actions of significance, authorizing a credentials manual expected to be followed by all assemblies doing credentialing (see above) and launching "Project Imagine" that would seek to envision a better way for the many ministry units of the Movement in North America to be related more closely for operational efficiency and mission effectiveness. My responsibilities were to be editor of the new Credentials Manual and recording secretary of Project Imagine's "Roundtable." My final report included this:

> The task necessarily would proceed in the prevailing context of two central and contrasting values treasured by the Church of God Movement. They form a pivotal paradox existing in this church body's DNA. It's the persistent attempt to champion and balance both freedom and accountability, taking human hands off the controls of God's church while also seeking to unite all believers for the greatest fulfillment of the church's mission.

The result of Project Imagine was modest, as one might have expected. It did launch a pilot program among certain assemblies on the West Coast of the United States. This was experimental and voluntary, typical of the Movement, but a hopeful beginning. The new credentials manual was adopted officially by all assemblies in the United States and eastern Canada by 2019. A new "Committee on Credentials" was elected by the Assembly and empowered to monitor the Manual's use and needed revision from time to time. It immediately became active and slowly accepted, despite initial nervousness about its very existence.

These seven arenas of tension have troubled the Movement in recent decades. Are they natural stress points that will resolve themselves with the passing of more time? Or are they problems that have deep roots and eventual consequences that are serious indeed for this Movement's future?

A small symbol of the potential seriousness was seen recently in Anderson, Indiana. Concerned persons had envisioned and finally brought into being a quality museum of the Movement's history. It was high-tech, featuring photos, artifacts, core themes, and beloved voices of the Movement, past and present. It was located in prime public space in the large Warner Press/Church of God Ministries complex adjacent to the Anderson University campus. The hope was that new generations would be exposed to this exciting story and inspired to carry it forward.

What happened? Relatively few came to visit. Then the Movement's large annual Convention moved away from Anderson and the historic building housing the museum was sold to a private company and turned into office and storage space for the general public. The "living" museum of the Movement died in the process. A fine archives of the history of Anderson University and the Movement as a whole does continue nearby as part of the Nicholson Library of the University, but the public presentation of that history is gone. It had fallen victim to limited interest and real estate realities. Does such a fate await the Movement itself if classic tensions are not handled well and soon?

Facing the Tensions

The often uncomfortable clashes of the Church of God Movement with its surrounding cultures have taken their toll. It's been a struggle for a Movement that hopes to remain free of obvious "denominational" controls that might regulate and protect its life.

The Movement often has found itself at odds with itself. All giving is voluntary and its many ministries usually seek funding from the same sources and act quite independently. The Movement's commitment to two opposing values has been at the base of the trouble. The values are *autonomy* (freedom) and *unity* (intentional togetherness). While both are deeply prized, living simultaneously and comfortably with both is virtually impossible at times. Beloved words from the song *The Church's Jubilee* voice the paradox:

> No earthly master do we know, to man-rule will not bow,
> But to each other and to God, eternal trueness vow.

The Movement sometimes has done exceptionally well at living up to the first line. Everyone is free to choose whatever seems right in his/her own eyes (Judges 21:25). The second line has been more problematic. Most pastors who would never tolerate chaos in their local settings have tended to tolerate it otherwise. When change or new programs are proposed, too often they are met with a defensive and even adversarial spirit. There's almost a caustic attitude toward any real leadership or plan of control beyond the local level.

In higher education, ministerial credentialing, biblical interpretation, and elsewhere in the life of the Movement, interfacing with the surrounding culture, secular and church, has brought significant tension. It has spawned opposing "camps" of Movement leaders who have strained the Movement's own unity, even as it has sought greater unity in the whole body of Christ.

In the 1930s it was the "Ohio Uprising" against the supposed "liberalizing" of the school in Anderson. In the 1940s it was the "Watchmen on the Wall" crusade that was highly critical of the *octopus* in Anderson, the perception that growing ministry agencies were strangling the church with new programs judged highly suspicious power moves of a few wayward ministers. In the 1970s there emerged the Pastors Fellowship, a "conservative" force, and the private publication of *Colloquium*, a fresh outlet for a "progressive" force.

The General Assembly was the natural point for these tensions to surface. It has adopted numerous resolutions on a wide range of subjects.[60] It convened a "Dialogue on Internal Unity" in 1981 to try to handle constructively the major tension that had emerged after an especially troubled 1980 Assembly. There had been a most provocative "Open Letter" from a pastor to all Movement ministers in the United States and Canada[61] and sharp debate about whether "inerrancy" was a necessary view of the Bible's inspiration. It was feared that the sharply divergent views would seriously jeopardize the unity of the Movement's ministry. A carefully crafted compromise saved the day.[62]

Big changes have reshaped the Christian and secular landscapes from the Movement's birth in 1880 to today. Is the Movement, in the midst of this shifting environment, still fighting long-defeated foes? Has it, and is it still, floundering in a vacuum because of the loss of a clear and strong vision of its own identity and mission? Have the cultures in which the Movement has had to live impacted negatively certain of its founding idealisms? How does the Movement continue to honor its own idealisms while caught in the uncertainty of its many paralyzing paradoxes?

NEEDED CONVERSATION AND ACTION

1. The launching vision of the Church of God Movement was heavily anti-denominational in nature. Is that nineteenth-century foe still a big danger to the church's integrity and mission? Is it the enemy the Movement should still strive against?

2. The Movement has spent much time and energy (and bad biblical interpretation) demonizing the Roman Catholic Church and its "harlot daughters" (Protestant denominations). What about "Vatican Council II" of the 1960s that attempted to bring much-needed reform to Roman Catholicism? Did the Movement's own "Project Imagine" help bring needed change to the Movement's current problems?

3. Is the Church of God Movement ready for its own high-profile reassessment? Is a reform Movement that has sought to separate itself from the downsides of human controls of church life now needing some of its own controls? Can God's Spirit work through as well as without organized church life?

4. What about the "pentecostal" and "ecumenical" movements now so prominent in the worldwide Christianity? They have addressed the two core concerns of the Movement, holiness of life and unity of the church. Since these worldwide movements have not been perfect in perspective or performance, should the Church of God Movement continue to be separated from them or should it become a contributing participant to help with their greater success?

5. The Movement, strongly opposed to establishing potentially self-serving institutions in its life, nonetheless has done so. There is the irony of a reform Movement creating institutions that ideally should not exist, and then grieving the occasional loss of one when it fails. How can such awkwardness be faced with courage and creativity in the future?

6. The Movement has been pressured to change in some ways in order to adjust to outside forces. Has this resulted in acceptable accommodation or unfortunate compromise? Speak directly to the issues of women pastors and full racial inclusion.

A BIBLICAL TRANSITION

FROM REMEMBERING FRANKLY
TO REBUILDING WISELY

It's hard to relate properly yesterday and tomorrow. There's a good biblical model worth remembering at this key time in the ongoing journey of the Church of God Movement. It's reported in Zechariah 2:1-5.

> Then I looked up, and there before me was a man with a measuring line in his hand. I asked, "Where are you going?" He answered me, "To measure Jerusalem, to find out how wide and how long it is." An angel came and said: "Run, tell that young man, 'Jerusalem will be a city without walls because of the great number of people and animals in it. And I myself will be a wall of fire around it,' declares the Lord, 'and I will be its glory within.'

In chapter one we focused on the importance of remembering and honoring yesterday, although with appropriate caution. In chapter two we recalled that the Church of God Movement was launched initially by individuals with a passionate relationship with Jesus Christ and a determination to address boldly the needs of God's church in their time. That love resulted in a powerful motivating vision of what the pioneers understood to be the Movement's divine call on behalf of God's people in end times.

In chapter three we learned that this originating vision soon faced considerable challenges, including questioning of its proper grounding. The loss that followed, as seen in chapter four, created a difficult vacuum and decades of awkward Movement life that has suffered from a lack of clear self-understanding of the Movement's nature and role in today's setting. Now we move from remembering to rebuilding, and we do so with important biblical guidance.

Elements of this Movement's original understanding of its call and cause have eroded, even virtually disappeared. Others have endured and still are urgently needed by today's Christian family worldwide—although sometimes only after some thoughtful redefining and refocusing. Some mission possibilities are appearing for the first time in very new environments. The Movement somehow must face and evaluate all of this change and newness, although it lacks any standing venues for doing such evaluating. Its historic *ad hoc* approach to the organizational life of the church remains one of its weaknesses.

The following chapters give attention to these old and new elements of today's message and mission of the Church of God Movement. While rooted in the Movement's yesterday, they are selected and sometimes re-shaped for the needs of today and tomorrow. Present challenges and op-portunities don't always allow a simple duplication of the Movement's past. We are blessed with a wonderful crowd of wise witnesses from the Movement's past and present.[63] We must draw on this fund wisdom without being limited to it. It's now time for the Movement to regroup, refocus, and boldly move on.

Following a time of struggle and loss, and now facing a new day, what should the Church of God Movement be doing? What's the best way for-ward? Many persons and events from yesterday really do deserve remem-bering and honoring, but there are past mistakes to be recognized, loss to be grieved, and the need to go forward on paths not traveled before. The Bible reports a similar circumstance and reviews the available op-tions for how to find a fresh start in a new time. Zechariah 2:1-5 is espe-cially helpful.

The Journey of the Jews

The Bible traces the long journey of the Jews trying to be God's people as called and intended. This journey is similar to that of the Church of God Movement in striking ways. Therefore, recalling the biblical experi-ence is worth the time. God's people always have struggled to under-stand and implement properly their special calling from God. This is seen throughout the Bible and across the generations of the Church of God Movement.

God has a people who have been chosen, called, and sent into this world on behalf of the world's redemption. The Jews followed the dra-matic calling of Abraham and believed in their special identity. Then came the challenge of finding the ways of defining and living out their specialness in a corrupt world. Over the generations the Jews persisted, experimented, turned inward, compromised, institutionalized, legalized, even fossilized. All this led to the eventual Exile of judgment and cleans-ing.

Fortunately, this biblical pilgrimage eventually came to include a grand return from the Exile and a chance to begin again. The problem then faced was deciding what to rebuild, and how and why. Should the proud but compromised yesterdays be resurrected or a new day faced courageously in a new way? What did God want in the new time?

The freed Jews, once back in Jerusalem, faced the urge to rebuild the old walls defensively. They also encountered an awareness that God was seeking for them a fresh identity, a different way of being God's chosen people on behalf of a lost world. It was really the original way that had been spoiled by centuries of faulty understandings and failed implementations.

As reported in Zechariah 2, what appeared to the returned Jews was the vision of a special tomorrow for God's chastened people. It would be a tomorrow featuring God's very character and mission being lived out by the chosen people *on God's terms*. The new day was not to be identical with the blueprints of the old city of Jerusalem or yesterday's journey of the Jews that had been much too self-centered. They had been like the original "come out" approach of the early Church of God pioneers. They had misjudged their being chosen as a divine call to an aloof separateness. That was now to be different.

Unfortunately, this fresh second-chance vision reported in Zechariah 2 would be largely ignored by the Jews in favor of the renewed pride of a rebuilt city with high defensive walls. There would be fresh legalism, an institutionalizing of how life for the faithful would be lived and how all "outsiders," the supposed unchosen, would be treated. That was hardly what the angel reported from God. The new Jerusalem was to be without walls, indwelt by God, outward-reaching, servant-oriented, and God-protected. God promised to be a wall of fire burning within the hearts of the chosen, and a pillar of Pentecostal fire flowing through them and showing the way for all others. God's people were to exist *for* others, not *against* them.

Here's great wisdom and warning for the future of the Church of God Movement. The flawed parts of yesterday have a stubborn way of persisting among God's chosen, causing them to focus their faith on the wrong things. That wrongness infected the returned Jews by evolving a wrong expectation of a coming Messiah who would protect and solve the persistent problems of the Jews. Surely, they falsely believed, God wants and one day will provide the very best for the chosen people in this world.

The Bible story moves on. The divine fulfillment of the messianic expectation eventually came, but in a form very different from what was wished and hoped. Most Jews rejected the Messiah when he came. Surely Jesus was not the real thing. He was a "suffering servant" who failed to throw off the hated Roman yoke. He accomplished God's ongoing work *in God's way* and called on his disciples, the chosen people of all times, to follow him, carrying their own crosses of potential suffering. The people of God were home from Exile with a second chance to get their calling right. Their choices were not all good ones.

Was the coming of Jesus a false blip in the ongoing journey of the Jews or the pinnacle of divine revelation? For those who believe that Jesus was truly God with us, the next stage of the journey of God's people is finding the cross-carrying way forward, the Jesus way into the world of today. Promises of worldly success are not offered, and building prideful holy cities for churchly defense must not be the agenda. The focus is to be on the unbounded ministry of the Spirit of Jesus who now is to be the church's life, provision, protection, and hope.

People of past exoduses and exiles are now to be "Pentecost People." The power and safety of God's people is to be true life in the Spirit and proper mission through the Spirit. These choices and opportunities are now facing the Church of God Movement.

Joining the Biblical Journey

The Church of God Movement originally rejoiced in being chosen by God, even being the final thrust of God's work in this world prior to the end of time itself. It now has faced the confusing complexities of world engagement, self-questioning, and even divine judgment. The time has come to rethink its post-Exile identity and mission. The call now is to face God's new day and do so *in God's own Jesus way*. Only people of Jesus' Spirit will be adequate for God's redemptive mission.

The Movement must hear an Isaiah-like grand announcement. It has been released from exile to come back home from Babylon. It's a wonderful starting-over opportunity. God announced through Isaiah, "When you're between a rock and a hard place, it won't be a dead end because I am God" (Isa. 43). This amazing opportunity comes only by God's grace and it carries new responsibilities.

The Movement faces a circumstance today much like what the returning Jewish exiles faced long ago when released from Babylon and returned to a ruined old Jerusalem. The remains of yesterday, good times and bad times, were strewn about, and the urgent questions were, and again are:

- How are yesterday, today, and tomorrow to be related properly?
- Is the once powerful holy city now hopelessly pathetic?
- Should God's people rebuild by using the blueprint of the old city?
- Where are the old boundary markers, and should they be moved?
- What should we be trying to wall in and wall out as God's faithful people?
- Should we focus on building defensive walls or neighborly relationships?
- Dare we face our world by being "suffering servants" like Jesus?
- Will we dare to sacrifice in fulfilling God's mission for our present time?
- Dare we live as "Pentecost People"? How do we figure out what that is?

The vision of Zechariah 2 remains an important guide—and warning. The arrival of the Spirit of Jesus is the necessary provision for the ongoing journey of the church. The past must be allowed to inform but not dictate the future. The wind of God will blow where it chooses. The new Jerusalem, today's church, should be a network of interdependent and united villages, diverse in their unity and defended not by walls of stone but by the presence and power of a surrounding ring of fire, God's indwelling Spirit.

Tomorrow must be a new day faced in new and relevant ways. More important than the details of the dwellings where God's people will live or the programs they will implement should be their focus on the Divine One. God is prepared to live in and empower God's chosen to serve in the Jesus way, through the agency of the Spirit, for the sake of today's lost world.

The writer to the Hebrews gave important advice now critical for the Church of God Movement. "Remember those early days after you first saw the light? Those were the hard times! Kicked around in public, targets of every kind of abuse. Nothing set you back. So don't throw it all away now. You need to stick it out, staying with God's plan. We're not quitters who lose out. We'll stay with it and survive, trusting all the way" (10:32ff, *The Message*).

We've recalled the daring and difficulties of the pioneer days of the Movement. There certainly is no desire to throw that all away. But what is God's plan for the way ahead? The chapters to follow attempt at least beginning answers. They gather up important threads from the Movement's journey to date, evaluate and sometimes restate them, and attempt to weave them into the beginnings of a new Spirit-tapestry to help guide the Movement's coming tomorrow.

We seek the Spirit's help as this delicate weaving proceeds. We recognize that much at the heart of the beginnings of the Church of God Movement seems very relevant yet today. Contemporary New Testament scholar N. T. Wright put it well in his address to the 2017 Lausanne-Orthodox Initiative:

> Holiness is fairly easy if you don't care about unity; you just split over every disagreement. Similarly, unity is fairly easy if you don't care about holiness; anything goes and we shrug our shoulders and ignore it. One of our biggest challenges, if we are to move forward in mission, is *the combination of unity and holiness.* The world will take no notice of a divided church. The world will take no notice of an unholy church.

Wright echoes loudly the heart and voice of the Movement's Daniel Warner in the late nineteenth century!

Chapters eight and nine to follow attempt restatements of the holiness-unity theme for today's Movement. A life-changing personal immersion into God's amazing love (holiness) enables a unity among God's people that is focused, not on judgment of others, but on reaching out together to share that divine love.

The other following chapters pick up additional elements of the Movement's teaching heritage that are crucial for the church today. Granted, they are reshaped somewhat, giving up old language that no longer communicates and old implementations that no longer are relevant. The concern is for enduring truth, not preserving the words and culture that carried it in another time and place. Rebuild Jerusalem, yes, but not necessarily with the old blueprint!

Chapter 5

THE BIBLE, SPIRITUAL EXPERIENCE, AND DOCTRINE

A central strength of the Church of God Movement has been its constant affirming that "the Bible is our only creed." Doctrines are to be formed through diligent and intensive interpretation of Scripture. Once formed, they are to remain tentative, subject to further biblical review.

But we must not think that the Movement's pioneers did all the necessary Bible interpretation and doctrinal formation. Each generation must search the Scriptures for itself if the Bible is to be our *only* rule of faith. And if it is, what about the importance of spiritual experience, also crucial to the Movement's understanding of how to gain true religious knowledge?

We've seen the Church of God Movement's early dramatic vision (chapter 2), observed its partial demise (chapter 3), and reviewed some of the paradoxes it's lived with for generations (chapter 4). Now it's rebuilding time for the Movement, hopefully guided by the vision in Zechariah 2.

Following his original "commission" from the Lord, Daniel Warner, the Movement's primary pioneer, spent the rest of his life trying to find ways of making that illumination fruitful in bringing the church back to God's intention. Unfortunately, his life was short and little was accomplished in structuring effective ministries for the long-term future—which Warner doubted would even exist.

Our current purpose, then, is to take up his innovative task. We look for key insights that deserve to be enduring building blocks rooted in the Movement's yesterday. Once identified, each may be altered somewhat to be adequate for today and tomorrow. All must arise from serious consideration of the voice of the Spirit as heard in the text of revealed Scripture. All must honor the Movement's past without being limited to it.

The Bible and God's Spirit

"Back to the Blessed Old Bible" is a slogan that's always been close to the heart of the Church of God Movement. The Bible is the Spirit-inspired record of God with us, especially in Jesus. To say the Bible is "inspired" means that, in spite of its great age and diversity, in the Bible's text we can hear God speaking to us in life-changing ways. It's text is infused with the breath of God and has the power to bring us into a redemptive relationship with the living God. "The Bible is the literary location where God continues to speak to us for the purpose of bringing us to faith and offering us newness of life."[64]

At the Movement's centennial in 1979-80, its seminary, Anderson University School of Theology, produced a *WE BELIEVE* statement with this underlying conviction: "We do not seek to be theological innovators, emphasizing as our group distinctive any doctrine or practice at the expense of losing perspective on the whole of revealed truth as it is centered in Christ and normatively set forth in Scripture (Eph. 2:19-22)." That's wisdom for the future yet to be faced.

Church of God people have accepted biblical authority and then tended to read the Bible "through the lens of their experience."[65] Such reading is inevitable, we all do it, and it's highly valuable when that experience is rooted in personal renewal in the image of Christ by his Spirit. However, it's dangerous to rely on one's own experience in today's culture of extreme individualism. This danger highlights the importance of the church, the community of Bible readers.

Two things must be kept in mind when interpreting the Bible. First, while the Bible is authoritative, discovering its meaning involves careful reading enriched by the current witness of the Holy Spirit. Bible and Spirit are intimately connected. True understanding of the text requires the Spirit's inward ministry. God, the original Inspirer of the biblical revelation, is obviously in the best position to assist with its best contemporary understanding and application. Required are both the original *inspiration* of the writers and the current *illumination* of the readers. This illumination is closely related to one's spiritual experience and sensitivity, but it must not rely only on these.

There's a second critical requirement. We must not read and interpret alone and without relevant knowledge. Awareness of the original Bible settings and languages are of great assistance, and so is the history of the text's interpretation across the centuries. That brings the church into the interpreting picture.

A particular problem today is the high valuing of individualism. When that is coupled with the large emphasis on freedom in the heritage of the Church of God Movement, it's so easy to have personal experience and knowledge (or lack of it) speak to us authoritatively, instead of the voice of God speaking through the biblical revelation in the context of the church. The church and its unity are very important. We are to read the inspired text, checking and teaching each other. That includes individuals within a congregation and church traditions within the wider body of Christ.

Our corporate reading of the Bible is a safeguard against strictly individual understandings. Such reading *together* should include the saints of yesterday as well as those of today. "Tradition," a frequent drag against progress, can also be a critical resource to check present perceptions that can be currents of the day more than wisdom from God.[66] The Movement has been so resistant to denominational traditions and historic church failures that sometimes it has failed at quality biblical interpretation. This failure has come either from leaning singularly on the Movement's own reading tradition or, because of valuing individual autonomy so highly, no reading tradition, just an individual's perspective.

Identified in the life of the Movement have been three "doctors of the church," Earl L. Martin, Adam W. Miller, and Albert F. Gray. The Movement placed great confidence in these three teacher-ministers "because they offered their work to the church in an idiom grounded *in experience*. The church understood that idiom as its own and prized it as the truth of Christian faith and discipleship."[67] There is wisdom in placing confidence in outstanding individuals when they are of the quality of these three, but sometimes even these must be put alongside biblical insights from other Christian traditions and cultural contexts.

One book co-authored by a Church of God scholar speaks this way of the "Scripture principle." "The Bible is the primary and fully trust-worthy canon of Christian revelation, the reliable medium for encountering and understanding the God who seeks to transform all persons who read the sacred text into the image of Jesus Christ. The Bible is the standard by which to shape and evaluate the church's theology, life, and mission."[68]

Note that the "experience" of being conformed to Christ is central. Doctrine does not come pre-formed in the Bible. It is shaped best in the process of biblical encounter and spiritual formation, particularly when biblical interpretation and growing discipleship happen together within the community of believers. One is able to hear best the voice of Christ's Spirit the more one is alive in Christ personally and immersed in the Christian community.

Since theological teachers in the Movement have valued the Wesleyan heritage of Christianity in particular, it's worth noting an emphasis of John Wesley. He believed that the biblical materials have a basic "particularly salvation" purpose. "In God's presence, I read his book for this end, to find the way to heaven." Quality reading of the biblical text requires the immediate *illumination* of the reader by the Spirit, the same Spirit who *inspired* the original writers. The holiness of the reader is key to understanding properly the holy Bible given by the holy God.

The Bible is not a simple record of truth claims, an encyclopedia of religious instruction that's permanently molded in fixed words and doctrines that disciples of Christ are to learn and believe exactly as recorded. Limited humans did the original writing and editing of the biblical text, and that's quite evident in the text.

But the human involvement is not the whole of the truth. The un-limited God was also active in the original writing and editing so that the end result is a human production that carries a Divine stamp of approval. As was true with the original writers and editors, proper understanding the Bible today requires of the reader a fresh relationship with the ever-living God.[69] That relationship is best developed inside God's community, the church, and not outside on one's own.

The Bible is a complex reality often misunderstood and misused. It's the crucial record where Word and Spirit are actively relating, where human writers and the Spirit's ministry join, enabling insight into the very heart of God. The Spirit still lives in this special written record to engage and transform the seeking and humble human of any day. The key word is "transform." The primary purpose of biblical revelation is not to be a treasury of Christian viewpoints on all subjects that might interest a reader. Rather than *informational*, the Bible's primary purpose is *formational*, guiding the reader into life and ministry in the image of Jesus Christ.[70]

God's Spirit takes what once was recorded in a very different time, setting, and language and brings it alive in the reader's heart, mind, and setting. The Spirit, especially in the context of the whole church, makes possible three things. They are the proper understanding of the intent of the original writing, an overcoming of the cultural shifting and changed languages, and the realization of proper applications critical for life, theological formation, and church mission today.

From Bible to Doctrine

For the Church of God Movement, the theological basics of "orthodox" Christianity have always been assumed. Formalized "creeds," however, have been put in a secondary position, even vigorously opposed for two reasons. They often are used as humanly-devised tools of denominational division and they tend to violate the vital role of spiritual formation, replacing the present work of God's Spirit with pre-set doctrines that are as much human creations as divine utterances.

The Bible does not provide a finished theology, but a path to the God about whom theology speaks. In the end, it's more important "Who" you know than "what" you think about various theological issues affirmed and often disputed among Christians. Jesus is the Subject and being rightly related to him through his Spirit is the most crucial matter. Truth lies deeply in restored relationship. In words often sung by Bible-reading Christians in search of a relationship with God:

> Beyond the sacred page,
> I seek Thee, Lord;
> My spirit pants for Thee,
> O living Word.

The joy of people in the Church of God Movement has come from their ability to testify to the reality of Christian truth being known "in the heart." Doctrinal summaries, while often honored, have been recognized as conditioned by the time of their formations. Formalized creeds too often were "political" decisions among Christian parties with contrasting viewpoints and under pressure to agree on some middle ground. Added to that has been the common use of creeds by denominations to fence in truth and wall out believers who think a little differently. The result has been the understandable hesitation of the Movement to champion any particular creed as "official" in its church life.

The Bible is the seedbed of truth; doctrines are understandings of that truth by particular groups of Christians at various times and settings in church history. Therefore, for the Movement proper Christianity is not merely supposed right thinking about theological issues. Christian faith must not be reduced to a debate about words that threatens to supplant experienced and lived spiritual reality. God's intended unity among believers will never come through full theological agreement but only through believers being spiritually formed together into the image of Christ. "The Bible certainly is a book to be believed; but even more, it is to be performed, practiced, lived."[71]

One episode among Movement leaders came close to violating this key stance. In 1980-81 a "battle for the Bible" debate was raging among "evangelical" Christians. It captured the attention of an especially conservative segment of the Movement's ministers. They began advocating loudly for a required acceptance of the "inerrancy" theory of understanding biblical inspiration, in effect "creedalizing" a much-questioned theological construct. They, of course, saw their effort as only insisting on the integrity and full authority of the Bible.

Anderson University School of Theology went into action, seeing great danger in the attempt to get the General Assembly of the Movement in the United States and Canada to pass a resolution affirming and even mandating the "inerrancy" approach to defining the inspiration of the biblical text. The Movement's seminary produced a special 1981 issue of its *Centering On Ministry* publication.

Faculty members wrote to clarify the issues, their history in the Movement, and the importance of avoiding the proposed vote in the General Assembly—which, ironically, by its very constitution, is not to function as a creed-making body. The resulting action of the 1981 General Assembly was carefully nuanced and wisely avoided "inerrancy" language when it said, properly linking the Bible's authority to the spiritual life:

> The Bible is without error *in all that it affirms*, in accordance *with its own purpose*, namely that it is "profitable for teaching, for reproof, for correction, for training in righteousness, that the man of God may be adequate, equipped for every good work" (2 Tim. 3:16-17, NAS), and it therefore is fully trustworthy and authoritative as the infallible guide for understanding the Christian faith and living the Christian life.

The Bible does not affirm a doctrine about itself that fits easily into the contemporary scientific mindset. It's a book of the ancient Middle East and not of the current Western world. We want it to fit our assumptions and expectations; it wants us to fit into the image of Christ by the renewing power of Christ's Spirit. The Bible is less a record of fixed doctrines and more the Living Word of God. That Word is to be read with care, within the body of Christ, guided by the illuminating instruction of God's Spirit, and interpreted best in accord with its salvation purpose.

In December, 1893, Daniel Warner, editor of the Movement's *Gospel Trumpet*, published an important article. It set the stage for what became and still should be the manner of the Movement's approach to biblical interpretation. Although the highly respected primary pioneer of the Movement, Warner claimed no reading and interpreting insight superior to his ministerial colleagues. Rather, he "continued to follow an emerging practice of interpretation that allowed for divergent views in a conversation that trusted the Spirit to lead the church into all truth."[72] We must trust the Spirit as we search the Scriptures together.

Keeping Bible Centered

The 1981 action of the General Assembly was wise in declaring that the Bible is "without error in all that it affirms." On occasion the Bible "reports" things it doesn't "affirm." It's fully dependable in accord with its own core purpose, bringing people back to the image of and life in Christ. It's core purpose does not include providing answers from heaven to satisfy contemporary curiosities about issues of astronomy, geology, evolution, economics, international politics, etc.

Also not included in the Bible's intention is providing pre-formed and permanently fixed "doctrines" to be memorized, mimicked, and mandated of each other. The truth of God is too personal and expansive to be captured fully in any human words or clever formulas, true and valuable as they may be. Rather than digging for doctrine in isolated biblical passages, believers should be focusing on what the Bible intentionally and clearly affirms throughout. Such focusing ensures that we stay centered on what the Bible has centered for us. We must avoid loving supposed law more than living the Christ-centered law of love.

The Movement has strayed here occasionally despite its anti-creedal stance. It has insisted on fixed views of the manner of baptism, a requirement of foot washing, the name of the church ("Church of God"), and a given scheme of eschatology, as though its current views on such matters are clear, intentional, and mandatory biblical teachings. The Movement must continue its traditional practice of biblical interpretation that allows divergent views in an ongoing conversation that trusts the Spirit of God to lead the church into all truth.

Let's review what the Bible definitely does affirm throughout. Four primary streams of biblical truth flow on or beneath the surface of the Old Testament text and then burst to the surface in the New Testament. They tell about the life-giving God who has chosen to be *with* us and *for* us troubled humans. This saving presence was first with Israel and ultimately appeared in the person, sacrifice, and resurrection of Jesus, and now in the ministry of Christ's Spirit.

God's revealing and saving presence is seen in four primary truth streams. They are thoroughly biblical and thus the proper building blocks for true Christian believing in any century, culture, or church setting. These biblical truth streams are:

Stream #1: <u>Church</u>. God has chosen a people with a special mission in the world. The choice is by grace and not because of any deserving. The chosen people are responsible for being the heralds of God's good news for all people. God has partnered first with Israel and now, through Jesus, with the body of Christ, the church.

Stream #2: <u>Sin</u>. What is the good news for all people in all times? Life is lived best in accord with God's created order and intended purpose. God has given freedom of choice that has been used badly—people choosing evil ("live" spelled backwards). The natural order of things has been disrupted. God has given the chosen people knowledge of the way back to God, and they are to receive it gladly and share it excitedly with others.

Stream #3: <u>Holiness</u>. All life is intended to be holy and pure in light of the holiness of the God who created and sustains life. God's chosen people are to reflect the divine life in their own lives through the transforming power and uniting love of God's Spirit. The chosen are to be changed, "sanctified," and model the divine likeness with each other and the world. The church is to be united by this common experience of renewal in the Spirit. Christ-likeness is essential for fulfilling credibly the church's calling in this fallen world.

Streaming #4: <u>Hope</u>. God enables a hope that sustains faithful believers, even in the face of difficult circumstances. This hope transcends the present time with its fragile institutions and practices that often work in opposition to God's will. The chosen people are called to herald the good news of available salvation for all people, made possible only by the grace of a loving God who was with us in Jesus the Christ and remains with us in his Spirit. This divine presence provides a sustaining hope for the present and for all eternity.

These four streams of truth flow throughout the Bible from the fountain of all truth, God. They comprise the heart of the biblical story and thus the basics of Christian belief. They are more living truth streams than fixed doctrinal statements. The biblical story is that God created, now has been with us in Jesus, remains with us in the Spirit of Jesus, and one day will conclude the history of this time-space world in judgment and justice. In this story of God's gracious Self-revelation one finds salvation, holiness, unity, mission, and hope.

God's people are to learn this story (engaging together in serious Bible study), grow in grace, mature in holiness, live in hope, and unite in mission for the salvation of all people. They are to rely on the dependable truthfulness of this biblical story and not stray into legalisms and build exclusive and divisive church institutions that tend to undercut and distract from the story's clear intention.

NEEDED CONVERSATION AND ACTION

1. The recovery of biblical authority has been a touchstone of the Church of God Movement. However, this central belief has become too much a slogan set to music, something more symbolic

than real. Recovery of the significance of the biblical message is essential for the Movement's renewal today. This will require fresh and disciplined Bible study. What can be done to launch this needed recovery?

2. Charles Naylor, close friend and admirer of the Movement's primary pioneer, Daniel Warner, said candidly in 1948 that Warner misinterpreted many biblical texts, especially in regard to "prophetic" biblical passages. Can we now be humble about our current understandings of the Bible and willing to read and think together as the whole church? Do you recall the key guidance given by Warner in 1893?

3. How can we avoid being blown about by current winds of supposed biblical thought when the average person in the pew is essentially illiterate biblically? Is it true that many preachers are not prepared or willing to do the hard work of serious biblical exposition from the pulpit? Who will speak up and do something about this? Formal theological education is not required for ministerial ordination in today's Movement. Is this acceptable?

4. Read again the lines just beneath the title of this chapter. If the Bible is "our only creed," and if the church gives little attention to serious Bible study, is the Movement now essentially creedless? If so, is it in danger of mindlessly accepting the biblical interpretations of the currently popular TV preachers?

5. The schools of the Movement originally were "Bible training" institutions. Today they have broadened their curricula considerably—for understandable reasons, of course, and with many wonderful results. Even so, many youth of the Movement are as close to being biblically illiterate as anyone else, and the universities of the church are pressured to offer courses of study that lead to good-paying jobs, and that's hardly biblical study. What's the way around this practical problem?

6. Note again the four central themes of clear biblical truth. Do you understand and accept these? Do you feel the need to add more as essential for believers? If so, are you leaning toward a doctrinal legalism that goes beyond the Bible's clear intent?

7. Are you individually or is a group you lead prepared to dig deeply into the pressing issues of biblical authority and interpretation? This is not an easy task, just one of central importance. Two major study sources are:
   a. *The Scripture Principle,* Clark H. Pinnock and Barry L. Callen, third edition, Emeth Press, 2009.
   b. *Bible Reading in Wesleyan Ways*, eds. Barry Callen and Richard Thompson, Beacon Hill Press of Kansas City, 2004.

THEOLOGY: BEYOND A CREEDAL PARALYSIS

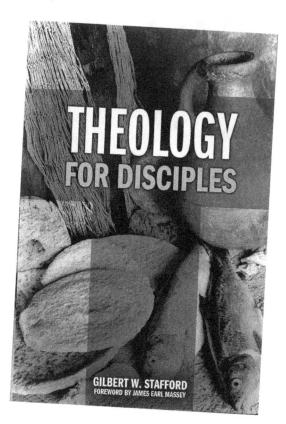

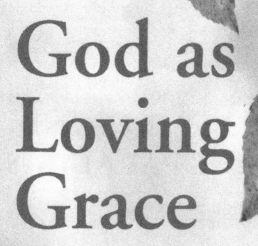

God as Loving Grace

The Biblically
Revealed
Nature and
Work of God

BARRY L. CALLEN

Chapter 6

To be bound thoughtlessly to complex theological creeds is a typical failure of Christianity. And yet, to avoid serious theological engagement and expression is hardly a viable alternative. Out of a sense of being paralyzed by a lack of theological understanding and consensus, the Church of God Movement has called for "a clearer, more relevant expression of the existing theological foundations upon which this Movement stands."[73] We join this call despite ongoing resistance to it.

Our purpose is not to go into detail about the theological history of the Church of God Movement. It's a complex story of various traditions of Christianity combining into what has become a distinctive theological mix.[74] Although the Movement's intention has been to be "creedless," in fact the Movement's theology is real and traceable historically, even if never put into finished form. My book *Contours of a Cause* traces these real "contours" that are definite if not fixed.

The Movement sometimes has assumed wrongly that it stands outside the denominational world of theological traditions. Such is hardly possible. The problem is that, while opposing a formalized theological stance, the Movement has tended to paralyze itself by not addressing its own theological tradition and refining it from time to time.

A Reluctant Theological Mix

The paradox (paralysis?) for the Church of God Movement is that it is a reform movement with strong theological convictions and yet a strong reluctance to formalize these convictions (fear of a denominational "creedalism"). F. G. Smith once attempted to have the Movement's General Assembly declare as authoritative the "standard literature" of the Movement. By that he meant only the biblical and theological material published prior to 1924, thus including his own *What the Bible Teaches* (1914) and excluding Russell R. Byrum's 1925 *Christian Theology* volume with which he was uncomfortable at points.

The Assembly in its wisdom resisted such a restrictive effort, judging such a declaration a "creedal" slamming of the door to further truth, as the denominations were routinely accused of doing. Smith, of course, intended to be protecting the truth that he judged central to the Movement's integrity. But this Movement has judged that neither Smith nor anyone else is to make a private judgment mandatory for all others.

The Movement, then, is always to be engaging, refining, and growing in its doctrinal thinking and expressions. Charles Naylor's classic song lyrics announce that, for the Movement, "the day of sects and creeds for us forevermore is past." While this points to the hoped-for end of the divisiveness of formalized creeds, it never meant that what one believes doesn't matter or shouldn't receive serious attention. Early Movement leaders cared deeply about right doctrine and never intended to launch a fellowship of free-thinkers. Sermons were full of doctrinal content.

F. G. Smith was a man of strong convictions shared widely and defended vigorously, although never allowed to be made "official." He once wrote this about the Movement: "We do not believe in extremism or fanaticism of any kind. We have no sympathy for strange or freak doctrines that are maintained only with subtle arguments, or with forced and unnatural interpretations of Scripture."[75] That said, he proceeded to be quite clear about his own convictions in *What the Bible Teaches* (1914), believing them to be natural biblical interpretations. Russell Byrum, Albert Gray, Kenneth Jones, Gilbert Stafford, Cliff Sanders, and I would believe much the same about our own interpretations (see the Bibliography). They carry many similarities without being reflections of each other.

To avoid an arid creedalism, statements of strong theological conviction need to be analyzed by others. Understandably, it was difficult for F. G. Smith to face the growing judgment that his approach to the Book of Revelation might be an "unnatural" interpretation. He loved the church and his motive always was to build it up. His later years were spent pastoring in Ohio, occasionally resisting the more "progressive" elements of the Movement's life and inspiring a young Lillie McCutcheon to carry on his "prophetic" emphases.[76] He also gave personal time to help rebuild confidence in the general church agencies in the troubled years of the 1940s. His role in the Movement's history was complex and significant indeed. His theological perspectives never were "official" despite being widely influential.

The "standard literature" attempt of Smith was not typical of the Movement's basic theological stance. The more typical anti-creedal concern has been that God is displeased with Christians using formalized and mandated doctrines to judge each other legalistically. Such judging builds unnecessary walls of division within Christ's body. Instead, believers are called to think carefully about the faith, confess their convictions openly, while being humble enough to submit current thoughts to the accumulated wisdom of the church over the centuries and to possible enrichment by the thinking of present brothers and sisters in the faith.

Believing, building, and refining doctrine should be an important, open, and ongoing process of church life. We are to believe strongly *and* humbly, being both clear *and* tentative. Thus arises the theological paradox of this Movement.

The Theological Stance in Brief

The mix that became the distinctive theological tradition of the Church of God Movement was commonly if informally understood by its older generations. However, it was rarely defined clearly or researched historically, and thus has not easily been known by future generations. This mix combines at least Reformationist, Restorationist, Wesleyan, Holiness, and Free-Church streams of Christianity, with these combined and nuanced in the rural culture of late nineteenth-century America. Theological work is never done in a vacuum, even if those doing the work are unaware of their partners in the process.

Two particularly strong theological influences on Daniel Warner, the Movement's primary pioneer, were the reforming thoughts of John Wesley and John Wienbrenner, fellow reformers of the eighteenth and nineteenth centuries. Here's how the Wesleyan tradition understands its place in the wider Christian community, obviously influencing the Movement's theological understandings:

> *Truly catholic*, we align ourselves with all those throughout the ages who are aligned with Jesus Christ.

Truly evangelical, we emphasize the gospel, the centrality of grace, and personal conversion.

Truly reformed, we believe that the church must undergo continual renewal and be constantly vigilant about its faithfulness to God.

The distinctive theological tradition of the Movement, reflecting such historic streams and emphases, intends to be "freshly faithful to a foundational past and newly determined to translate that past into the life of the present, without fear or favor."[77]

The Movement further intends to be biblical in focus and centered in the person of Jesus Christ. It also is to be "radical" by calling for an abrupt departure from the status quo of the wayward institutionalized churches that often have been in league with various political powers. The freedom gained by this departure is to yield release from theological creeds made mandatory by historic church bodies and sometimes also their related nations.

Christian allegiance is to be to God and God alone. It's *God's church*, not that of any nation or denomination. This commitment, always centered on Christ and nurtured by his Spirit, is to be guided by the Bible, the narrative that presents the truth story. It's to be enabled by the Spirit, the presence and power of truth. The result is understood by the Movement to be fully "orthodox," that is, in the mainstream of Christian belief.

As F. G. Smith said, there is to be nothing strange, no novel theological twists, just a return to the apostolic foundations of the faith, back to what always has been biblical and basic. The theological goal envisioned by the Movement is a return to being submissive to the sovereign God known in Christ and interpreted in the biblical narrative as enabled by the ministry of the Spirit. This narrative is fixed, but its theological expressions are fluid.

This Movement has been "thoroughly *catholic* in the breadth of its whole-church vision. It has been clearly *protestant* in its insistence on proper Christian identity by faith alone through Christ alone. And it has been genuinely *radical* in its insistence on real change in believers (holiness) and in the church (unity) as a result of God's grace and as evidence of the presence now of the kingdom of God."[78]

Convictional, Not Creedal

There's a paradox at the heart of the Movement's theological tradition. It's essential but difficult to maintain. Christian disciples are to be vigorously convictional, believing strongly in the grace of God that can alter life itself. They also are to avoid intellectualizing their convictions into formalized and mandatory creeds.

Why this avoidance? Truth exceeds the power of mere words to capture. The heart of Christian identity involves *experiencing* and *living* the truth, not exhaustively defining and explaining it. While truth certainly is believed to be objective reality, it also is understood to be personal, relational, dynamic, and contextual.

Christian truth is beyond the limits of full human understanding and often is distorted by being forced into the bounds of a given church tradition or theological statement—the typical approach of a Pharisee. While there is only one biblical revelation, understanding that revelation is necessarily partial and progressive. Because of truth's complexity (try explaining the "Trinity" of the one God), it's best to follow the Hebrew way seen often in the Bible itself. This way has been called a "propensity for paradox."

This biblical pattern, this propensity, is the willingness to leave unresolved the mysteries that exceed human language and full understanding. Believers always must be humbled by what God said to Job after he had demanded full explanation of his troubles. God said in response, "Why do you talk when not knowing what you're talking about? Where were you when I created the earth? Tell me since you know so much!" (Job 38).

Movement people have aspired to be "lovers of the truth," questing for the full truth as it is in Christ, yet without claiming any finality of full theological understanding. They have sought the narrow middle road of being clearly convictional without being narrowly creedal, hoping to be "conservative" and "orthodox" without being divisively "denominational" or narrowly "fundamemtalist." A fundamentalist insists on simple and clear answers to even the biggest questions, and sometimes winds up confidently championing half-truths—one way to define "heresy." The quest is always for "more light," for being both convictional and humble about one's beliefs. After all, our beliefs are always by faith and not full sight.

Proper as is this cautious approach to truth, it easily can lead to an awkward creedal paralysis. People want to be clear about what the truth is, and usually they revert to writing down in definitive statements precisely what they think. Usually they go on to expect others to agree. This tendency soon appeared in the Movement, although what has been written has never been formally declared "official" truth for all believers. One book came close for several generations.

F. G. Smith's book *What the Bible Teaches* tended to standardize the Movement's teaching early in the twentieth century. It gave the Movement "a theological spine which welded us together. As time went on it became a standard source of doctrine, the centerpiece of every church library, and the esteemed possession of almost every saint's home. In time it became the primer for every candidate for ordination and the standard of orthodoxy by which he or she was judged."[79]

This Smith book, however, soon was supplemented and in various ways even countered by other theological works, particularly Russell R. Byrum's *Christian Theology* (1925, 1982), Albert F. Gray's *Christian Theology* (1944-46), my *God As Loving Grace* (1996, 2018), Kenneth Jones's *Theology of Holiness and Love* (1995), Gilbert W. Stafford's *Theology for Disciples* (1996, 2012), and Cliff Sanders's *The Optimism of Grace* (2016). While all of these have been widely accepted, none has ever been considered "official" in the Movement. Rather, they have been viewed as the best works available at a given time and by the best thinkers of that time.

The Movement's 1963 All-Board Congress and Planning Council was convened to facilitate wide discussion on crucial issues then being faced by the Movement as a whole. Its Findings Committee summarized the results, including:

> We call for a clearer, more relevant expression of the existing *theological foundations* upon which this Movement stands.... Our witness must begin with a more adequate demonstration of what we teach, remembering that unity is not intellectual uniformity. While as a church we need to know *who* we are, and *why* we are, we should *not* be setting up distinctives in the denominational sense.

Note this attempt at a middle road that's easier to map than travel. The Movement urgently needs more theological clarity, but it must have its limits.

According to the Movement's theological tradition, there never is to be a denomination-like set of fixed theological "distinctives." Determining clarity without fixity is a difficult task indeed. The Movement is resistant to having a creed of its own, and also increasingly aware that it needs more clarity of its treasured convictions. This is the paradox of being convictional but not creedal. Is this paradox threatening to be a crippling paralysis of the Movement?

Why a Creedal Paralysis?

The theological position of the Church of God Movement is clearly paradoxical. It's both vigorously convictional and yet very resistant to formalizing its convictional positions. The Movement claims "light on the church," a special vision of what God intends the church to be. This light cannot be identified with any existing sect or denomination or even reform movement. The Movement's early call was for Christians to "come out" of the denominational system altogether and reside as one in the revealed light of an open fellowship of the "saints." To be "open" is to be convictional and also flexible in those convictions.

One key understanding of the Movement has been clear enough, even if not formalized. The church is to be *holy*. How? By its members being holy and then forming the sacred family of the saints joyously together in fellowship and mission. God's ultimate will is a single, united, and visible church. This one church should not be bound by formalized restrictions of human devising but have the quality of constant openness. Since the Spirit of Christ continues to be present in the family, revealing fuller understandings and current applications of biblical truth, formalizations of theology should be avoided. They tend to be partial, premature, divisive, and unnecessary obstacles to the ongoing work of the Spirit.

Anti-creedalism always has been part of the tradition of the Movement. It's been insisted that even the most central of theological convictions should not become institutionalized. There must be an openness to ever more "light" and a willingness "to walk into the light beyond what she or he currently has."[80] Each generation must rethink its understanding of doctrine to avoid the trap of adopting blindly theological positions merely because of tradition, including the Movement's own tradition.

Here's an important insight. "The pioneers of the Movement were not reaching back to tradition; they were reaching out to divine truth. When dealing openly and honestly with Bible truth, we have no reason to be fearful of asking penetrating questions about what we believe and why we believe it. Truth can stand the test!"[81] Openness to "more light" is the courageous and correct way to go.

Theological creeds are time-bound and culture-bound human constructions. They must not become a test of salvation or fellowship. Even so, they do inform, guide, and instruct, and the Movement never has been a group of free thinkers with an "anything goes" attitude toward the central truths of biblical revelation (see chapter five). The problem has been the stance of being caught between wanting to be full of strong, biblically-informed conviction and also wanting to avoid shutting off the avenues of growth in understanding and unnecessarily dividing the body of Christ and impeding the ministry of the Spirit.

Sadly, the fear of "creedalism" has been allowed to undercut the Movement's willingness to live in the open with its strongly-held beliefs. Only a handful of serious theological works have been produced in the Movement's history (see the Bibliography). Only a few times have there appeared formalized theological statements, and these usually were forced into being in times of crisis in the Movement's life.

For instance, Anderson College felt obligated around 1930 to produce a formal statement of the school's theological beliefs. It was a time of high tension, with many ministers accusing the school of not being true to the Movement's historic beliefs. Then the same campus produced a *"WE BELIEVE"* statement on the occasion of the centennial celebration of the Movement in 1979-80. There was a theological vacuum at this critical time in the Movement's history, someone needed to take the initiative, and the campus president, Robert H. Reardon, wanted it to be the School of Theology, the seminary of the Movement.

The call for more theological clarity again has become frequent in recent years. The All-Boards Congress in 1963 was one call (see above). The "Project Imagine" Roundtable in 2017-18 reported this: "While some structural change is clearly needed, no structural change can be the full solution to the present challenges. Beneath the obvious structural concerns lies the core need of clarifying the Movement's present identity and mission. A clear 'why' enables a workable 'how.' Such missional understanding of the Movement has eroded in recent decades and must be reclaimed."

There has been significant erosion. A large percentage of those attending today's congregations of the Movement has little or no awareness of the Movement's specific theological heritage or particular reforming mission in relation to the larger Christian church. Many pastors are themselves not especially versed theologically and would hesitate to stress theology in their preaching. Anything "heavy" might not be welcomed and might even offend some. Anyway, isn't the goal church growth and not thought uniformity?

When theological uncertainty is added to the widespread biblical illiteracy in the churches today, the challenge is clear. Pastors of the Movement need to engage without apology in teaching ministries. The subjects must focus on biblical content and theological essentials. Uniformity of thought should not be the goal, and denominational divisiveness needs to be avoided. Even so, failure here surely will allow the church to drift without a backbone and open the people to every wayward wind of doctrine that is broadcast or streamed their way.

What Should Ministers Believe?

Here's a key question troubling today's Church of God Movement. What is necessary for its ministers to believe? The common answer is the Bible, of course, all of it and nothing contrary to it. That's the ideal and the dilemma. It tends to mean anything classically thought of as "orthodox," and possibly anything that any Bible-believing community currently affirms. Is that the Movement's distinctive theology, to believe anything that anyone honestly thinks is biblical? The reluctance to be clearer than that is what we might call the Movement's "creedal paralysis."

This paralysis is seen particularly in the area of the Movement's modern-day ministerial credentialing practice. What is required theologically of all ordination candidates in the United States and Canada? The answer is found in the 2019 edition of the *Credentials Manual* authorized by the General Assembly. No standard is set forth as a common basis of belief other than the general teaching heritage of the Movement, which is not clearly defined.

Several affirmations are made. One highlights the Movement's emphasis on spiritual "experience" for church membership and a proper approach to theology. There is a caution stated. "Theological understanding can never rest on intellectual investigation alone. True theologizing cannot be done by the unspiritual person, since such a person lacks the insight provided by the presence and wisdom of the Holy Spirit."

Another affirmation is made. "It is not enough to set forth by rote a few creedal-sounding statements that appear traditional. It is only enough to have a broad foundation of theological method and conviction that encompasses, in principle at least, all the issues of life as they pertain to the nature and activity of God."

What is enough for ministers theologically, beyond a broad foundation of theological method? It's said to be merely this: "Although the Church of God honors theological freedom within the bounds of biblically-based belief, those to whom vocational credentialing is granted are expected to hold persuasions that are in general agreement with the teaching tradition of the Church of God."

Again, the Movement's teaching tradition is noted but not elaborated. All candidates for vocational credentialing are asked to prepare a written statement of their beliefs regarding sixteen subjects and then discuss this writing with examining colleagues. The list of subjects reflects theological topics of particular sensitivity to the Movement, including:

Whether a candidate's responses to these subjects is adequate is left to the judgment of the examining credentials committee, and the views of such committees have been known to vary from assembly to assembly and time to time.

➢ The nature and authority of the Bible;
➢ The nature of the church and its membership;
➢ The Holy Spirit's cleansing and gifting in the believer's life;
➢ The nature and importance of Christian unity;
➢ The status of women in ministry and leadership;
➢ The second coming of Jesus and its relation to present ministry.

This openness to honest theological variation is an example of the Movement's ideal of unity without uniformity. But is it also a hurtful creedal paralysis? Is it the best way to ensure the freedom of the Spirit to teach as God sees fit, or is it an open door to a likely theological chaos? See the following chapter for suggestions on addressing these important questions.

NEEDED CONVERSATION AND ACTION

1. A group's believing tradition comes from somewhere, and the several sources of the believing tradition of the Church of God Movement are now quite well known. Does such awareness make any difference? Does the Movement believe anything brand new in the Christian tradition?

2. Is or is not the Movement theologically Wesleyan, holiness, amillennial, and Trinitarian? How many of us know what these words mean? Should we know? Would knowing really make any difference in our Christian witness and relationships?

3. If "the day of sects and creeds for us forevermore is past," what does that mean for what Movement people are to believe? It surely doesn't mean, and was never meant to mean, to believe anything one chooses.

4. The Movement urgently needs more theological clarity about its teachings, but clarity that has its limits. How can we establish clearer theological foundations, confessionalism, and yet resist the problems of creedalism?

5. This Movement has been catholic in the breadth of its whole-church vision, protestant in its insistence on proper Christian identity by faith alone through Christ alone, and radical in its insistence on real change in believers (holiness) and in the church (unity). Are these three characteristics building blocks of an acceptable "confessionalism"?

6. It appears that the current requirements for ministerial ordination in the Movement are not very specific, mandatory, or implemented in the same way from one credentialing assembly to another. Is this really the case and, if so, is it acceptable? Should (can) ministers of the Church of God Movement believe a range of things theologically?

7. Discussed in this chapter is a "creedal paralysis." What does this mean? Can freedom of theological thought be an open door to an unacceptable foolishness of thought?

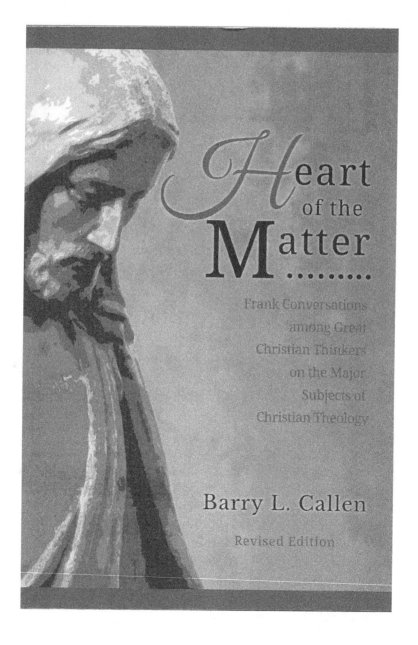

SHARING THE MOVEMENT'S THEOLOGICAL TREASURES

There are theological treasures in the teaching tradition of the Church of God Movement worthy of sharing with the whole of today's Christian community. There also is an obligation to share them or the Movement will fail to play its reforming role under God. What are these treasures? Is there enough confidence in them to encourage their being shared well beyond the bounds of the Movement?

Having recognized in the last chapter the theological paralysis caused by the Church of God Movement's stance of non-creedalism, we now move beyond this stalemate in search of constructive paths ahead.

Are there theological treasures resident in the teaching tradition of the Movement worthy of sharing with the whole of today's Christian community? Surely there are, and surely there is obligation to share them. Otherwise, this Movement will fail to play its reforming role under God. So we begin by highlighting the teaching tradition of the Movement, looking for the treasures worthy of sharing. When found, the hope is that they will be shared humbly for the good of the wider church, with the Movement also being prepared to benefit from the sharing of others.

The Movement's Theological Tradition

The Church of God Movement has not been a theologically rich one, at least not in the sense of producing a considerable volume of fresh theological literature. It has, however, maintained a rather consistent set of theological commitments, even if held and communicated only informally.

Five theological stances follow.[82] They do not appear in creedal form, but nonetheless are fundamental to the Movement's understanding of the faith and the church's mission.

1. The Church of God Movement is a worldwide reforming body dedicated to returning to central biblical teachings, serious Christian living, and reconciling this fallen world by the love and power of God.

2. Desiring to remain open to the fullness of God's truth and avoid further dividing of the church, this global Movement steers away from developing its own denominational distinctives. The preference is partnership in common cause with all believers on mission today.

3. Honoring Jesus Christ as Head of the church, the Movement desires to be a biblical people, a gathering of believers transformed by the grace of God and committed to building up the one church of God as it cares for the lost of the world and the creation itself.

4. The church is understood to be the body of truth-seeking pilgrims who have found the Way (Christ) but know that they have not yet arrived at comprehensive understanding. Accordingly, this Movement is a global body of believers that resists church organizations and creeds when they become humanly-devised barriers between believers and obstacles to fulfilling together the mission of the church.

5. Truth is to be *experienced* and not merely understood intellectually. Truth is to be *practiced* in sacrificial ministry and not merely cherished in formulas, buildings, and books. The beliefs of this Movement are understood to be thoroughly biblical and truly "orthodox." No special revelations are claimed beyond the Bible itself and the Spirit's ministry of properly interpreting the biblical revelation.

Given these five foundational stances, a proper approach to theological understanding in general begins with truth's foundation, the Bible's presentation of the Trinitarian God.[83] Note the following graphic that depicts an "orthodox" presentation of God as affirmed in the major Christian creeds and always assumed by the Church of God Movement.[84] The Trinitarian God is the focus of all biblical revelation and thus the center of all Christian believing.

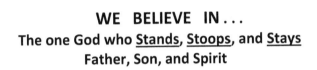
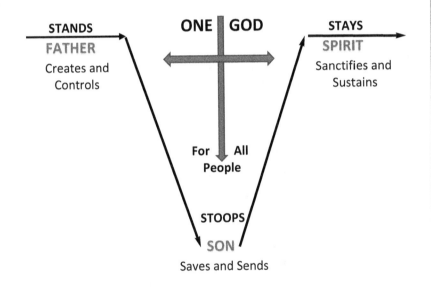

WE BELIEVE IN . . .
The one God who <u>Stands</u>, <u>Stoops</u>, and <u>Stays</u>
Father, Son, and Spirit

STANDS   ONE | GOD   STAYS

FATHER   SPIRIT

Creates and   Sanctifies and

Controls   Sustains

For | All
People

STOOPS
SON
Saves and Sends

The Fountainhead, the <u>Father:</u>
God **Stood** before time.

The Fulfillment, the <u>Son:</u>
God **Stooped** savingly into time.

The Follow Through, the <u>Spirit:</u>
God **Stays, Sanctifies, Unifies,** and
Sends until time is no more!!

Three Theological Basics

The membership of the General Assembly of the Church of God in the United States and Canada is limited to those judged by the Assembly to be "adhering to the general principles to which the Assembly itself is committed." Three such principles have been identified either by direct Assembly resolution or its common practice. See the related Assembly resolutions of 1981 and 1985 in the book *Leaning Forward* (2019). In brief, these theological principles are:

1. The **LORDSHIP** of Jesus Christ (Col. 1:15-20; Heb. 1:2-3). Said the General Assembly:

   > "Any inter-church body involved in a relationship with national ministry bodies of the Church of God Movement should be committed publicly to the divinity and lordship of Jesus Christ. He is central to the meaning and mission of the church." This statement is essential New Testament teaching. A current and related emphasis of the Movement is that "Jesus is the Subject!"[85]

2. The authority of God's **WRITTEN WORD** (2 Tim. 3:16). Said the General Assembly:

   > "The Bible truly is the divinely inspired and infallible Word of God. The Bible is without error in all that it affirms, in accordance with its own purpose, namely that it is "profitable for teaching, for reproof, for correction, for training in righteousness, that the man of God may be adequate, equipped for every good work" (2 Tim. 3:16-17, NAS), and it therefore is fully trustworthy and authoritative as the infallible guide for understanding the Christian faith and living the Christian life." The Bible, in effect, is the Movement's creed, all of the Bible and nothing contrary to it.

3. The central roles of the **SPIRIT OF GOD**. They are to teach about the meaning of Jesus' lordship, enable a correct reading of the Bible (Jn. 14:26), and inspire the proper manner of implementing the life and ministry of the church in each time and place. The ministry of the Holy Spirit is basic to the teaching heritage of the Church of God Movement and thus of its General Assembly.

The 1986 General Assembly's acceptance of a major study report on "glossolalia" (speaking in tongues) was a pivotal theological action. Included among the affirmations of this report was this: "An infilling of the Holy Spirit and an in-depth life in the Spirit are crucial to the maturing of individual Christians and to the accomplishment of the mission of the church in every age. A lack of the power of Pentecost explains much of the emptiness which the current church renewal and charismatic movements are seeking to fill."

Now come what have been called the five theological "non-negotiables." They don't represent any authoritative voice of the Movement beyond that of the current General Director, Jim Lyon. Even so, they were originated in 2013 by the leaders interviewing him for his major leadership role. Then in 2019, on the occasion of his ratification for a second term, he repeated them with passion to that General Assembly. They are:

First: **JESUS IS LORD**. The singularity, exclusivity, and divinity of the one Lord Jesus stand tall. The Bread of Life. The Water of Life. The Lamb of God. The Way, the Truth, and the Life. The one Mediator between God and humankind. The Lord of lords, The King of kings. The Son of Man. The Son of God. The Word become flesh. The Name at which every knee shall bow. *Jesus is the Subject.*[86] This defines us (the Movement).

Second: **HOLINESS**. The Person, work, and power of the Holy Spirit are fundamental to who we are as a people. We unabashedly own the truth that the Spirit can transform us, possess us, equip us, and empower us. It is the work of the Holy Spirit that makes us holy, sets us apart for sacred service, and seals us for eternity's sake. It is the Spirit who convicts us of sin and enables us to overcome sin. It is the Holy Spirit who can breathe supernatural gifts into us, for Jesus' sake. The Spirit is the Comforter promised by Jesus and the witness of our redemption. This defines us (the Movement).

Third: **UNITY**. We are a people called by God to be a catalyst for Christian unity, believing that the division of the body of Christ is hell's greatest weapon to thwart heaven's ends in this world. We are convinced that the splintering of the body is not the Lord's work but the enemy's. We believe that hell trembles at the prospect of a people united, redeemed by the blood, and possessed by the Spirit. Unity is not for us an also-ran on the to-do list of God, but a primary driver of who and why we are called out. It defines us (the Movement).

Fourth: **THE GREAT COMMANDMENTS**. Love God with your whole self, and love your neighbors as yourself. The Scripture tells us that this is the sum of the Law and the Prophets. When a teacher of the Law sought to test Jesus (Luke 10), asking, "What must I do to have eternal life?" Jesus asked him what he read in the Scriptures. When the man replied with the Great Commandments, Jesus approved, saying, "You have answered well; do this and you will live." As a people in pursuit of holiness, the Great Commandments clothe us. They define us (the Movement).

Fifth: **THE SUPREMACY OF SCRIPTURE**. We are a people of the Book, the Good Book, the Holy Bible, the Old and New Testaments, supernaturally inspired, preserved across time, cultures, and continents, delivered to us, useful for reproof and instruction in righteousness. The Scripture is our ultimate field of inquiry and judgment, the measure of conduct, faith, and practice. Whatever the question, whatever the test, whatever comes before us, in the end, it is the Scripture, above all other disciplines, that informs and defines us (the Movement).

Theological Perspectives for Global Sharing

The Church of God Movement is now a global fellowship. It is well positioned to be sharing with the broader Christian community several particular theological perspectives for the fuller health and mission effectiveness of the whole church. It should be doing so humbly, always remaining open to the shared perspectives of other Christian communities.

Here are six theological perspectives that I propose the Movement has and should be sharing. Such sharing would not be denominational arrogance but simple Christian stewardship. For the good of the whole church, each body of believers should cherish and share the particular understandings of biblical truth that it possesses, while remaining open to being enriched by the understandings of fellow believers of other Christian traditions. To be resisted are detailed and mandatory creeds that freeze understandings, discourage further learning, and are used as tools of hurtful division. The Movement's theological perspectives worthy of sharing are at least these:

1. Every body of Christians should focus on being a movement, avoiding the pitfall of excessive and corrosive church institutionalism. While organizing the church's work is necessary stewardship, claiming biblical finality for any organizational pattern or theological formulation is inappropriate. To be resisted in all sharing should be any "sectarian" spirit.

2. Bible-based theology is very important, but formalized theology isn't everything. Christian identity and church membership are to be rooted in Christian experience, persons being transformed into the image of Christ by action of the Spirit. Affiliation with a church body apart from new life in Christ is false church membership and poor theology. To be resisted is mere memorization of the classic creeds of the church, "orthodox" though they may be. True belief is to be experienced and practiced, not merely verbalized.

3. Christian faith and church life must be Spirit-oriented. Fearing possible emotional excess must not distract from this central truth of Christianity. The church was commissioned at Pentecost and is to be gifted, empowered, and governed by the Spirit of God, regardless of what organizational plan is employed or creed affirmed. To be resisted, however, is overly standardizing the subjective particulars of "Christian experience." The Spirit works as the Spirit wills.

4. Unity among all Christians is crucial to effective church mission. It will never be achieved by Christians agreeing on all points of theology and practice or by denominations flowing together into one master church organization. Christian unity is the natural fruit of common new life in the Spirit of Christ. Believers are to serve together as united instruments of the Spirit's ministry, regardless of the continuing diversity of thought and practice among them.

5. Expectations of end-time events should be tempered by humility and disciplined by the clear mandate of Scripture. That mandate of Jesus himself is to focus on the present mission of the church. Resisted must be speculations about the future that distract from

the ministry tasks and reconciliation possibilities immediately at hand. Jesus assured disciples of the future and then directed them to ministry tasks at hand. As Ann Smith, a contemporary saint of the Movement, says, "I live with expectancy, not expectations." To focus on particular expectations too often is an unacceptable weakening of active commitment to ministry now.

6.   The resurrection of Jesus was the beginning of God's ongoing project of infusing this fallen world with the transforming life of heaven. The church's mission is to model and witness to this new life in the Spirit, making disciples of the Master and assisting with their spiritual maturing and service deployment, all without national, racial or gender discrimination.

These six perspectives are not "denominational" but biblical and vital for the spiritual health and mission effectiveness of the church in every nation and culture and time. May the Church of God Movement become more willing to share them widely, boldly, humbly, and of course model them itself. And may God grant these perspectives a constructive role in the future ministries of the whole church worldwide.

NEEDED CONVERSATION AND ACTION

1. How important to you are clear theological foundations and understandings? How important do you believe they are in today's culture where individualism is so strong? How can we talk about theological truths to the youth of today and really be understood and appreciated by them?

2. Is there anything about the three theological basics from the Movement's General Assembly that you disagree with? Is there anything foundational that should be added to these three basics for a balanced view of Christian believing? Would adding to these be an unnecessary denominational creedalism?

3. Do the five "non-negotiables," as identified by the Movement's current General Director, fully address the theological truths critical to

the Church of God Movement? Have these always been believed by the Movement? Should they always be? Can you think of a sixth?

4. Are there theological truths that really are negotiable? How important is a common understanding of spiritual gifts, women in ministry, amillennialism, the name of the church, the manner of baptising, etc.?

5. Regarding the "six theological perspectives" listed above, are they truly central to the teaching tradition of the Movement? Are they so critical that they are worthy of sharing with Christians worldwide regardless of their church affiliations? Are you willing to help do this?

6. How does the identification and practice of the "ordinances" (the Lord's Supper, baptism, and foot washing) connect to basic theological truths? Does the New Testament instruct that these be practiced by all Christians and in the same way? How are these done at your church, or are they at all?

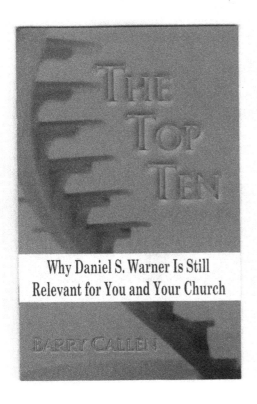

THE PRAYER
of Holiness-Hungry People

A Disciple's Guide to the Lord's Prayer

BARRY L. CALLEN

Chapter 8

HOLINESS: THE WHOLENESS OF ABUNDANT CHRISTIAN LIFE

The ongoing quest for holiness and unity in the church might be summarized as: (1) understanding the biblical meanings of Christian holiness; (2) experiencing that holiness in relationship and covenant with a holy God; and (3) finding in the wonder of this experience the vision, will, and power necessary to be truly God's children, united and on mission together in this lost world.

Christian spiritual formation is the process of people being formed into the likeness of Christ's character, and therefore agents of his redeeming love. Jesus should not only be our *Savior* but also our *Lord*, the One who forgives our past and launches our future. Holiness is the wholeness of this amazing process of new life in Christ.

When seeking to share the believing treasurers of the Church of God Movement with new generations of its own people and those of the wider church, one treasure is particularly important. Christian holiness has been understood by the Movement to be the heart of the abundant Christian life, and also the key to realizing the Christian unity required for effective witness to a lost world.

Law or Love?

While basic to the teaching tradition of the Movement, "holiness" remains difficult to define. Try this, an attempted definition that doesn't reflect an arrogant elitism ("holier than thou!') and doesn't lean on a set of negatives found in a church's legal code that supposedly defines exactly how a Christian must live in order to be "perfect" in God's eyes.

> To be "holy" is to have found and joyfully received God's gift of the abundant Christian life. Holiness is a human heart in which the Holy Spirit has been invited to dwell, filling it with a tender and constant love of God and others.

By contrast with this simple definition, "hyper religious" people tend to reduce holiness to following carefully the strict rules of life prescribed by a given religious group. Usually these rules are a collection of "don'ts"—holy people don't drink, smoke, dance, have a wandering sexual eye, etc. These rules sometimes are mere reflections of a given place and time. I know of one conservative "holiness" denomination whose Los Angeles members routinely act in some ways that never would be tolerated of its members living in the coal-mining towns of western Pennsylvania.

The New Testament moves in a very different direction. Love is highlighted rather than the technicalities of culture-bound law. It reflects what missionary Ann Smith did in the 1950s when crossing the Pacific Ocean to reach her missionary assignment in Japan. A crass businessman onboard came to respect her gentleness and Christian witness and finally asked her one day, "Ann, if I became a Christian, would I have to quit smoking?" He expected a blunt "yes!" Instead, she said, "The question is premature. First, allow yourself to get really acquainted with Jesus. Let him love and forgive and renew you. Then ask him your question, not me."

That's it. The joys of being in relationship with God are to come before the rules of God-like living. Paul defined holiness as the fruits that emerge from being in relationship with the Spirit of Jesus. They are attitudes before they are actions. "The fruit of the Spirit is love, joy, peace, forbearance, kindness, goodness, faithfulness, gentleness and self-control. Against such things there is no law" (Gal. 5:22-23).

Wanting to have sins forgiven, and nothing more, isn't enough. Half-hearted commitment to Christ won't do. The public today resists the shallow and obviously inauthentic. People are tired of petty lines of demarcation that divide Christians from each other over local rules and personal biases. What is longed for is a witness that transcends church institutionalism. There must be evidence of actual new life in Christ that transforms individuals, unifies God's family, and sends its members together on loving and serving mission.

And "loving" is the key word. Sins forgiven is the important beginning of the Christian meaning of "salvation," but only the big beginning. Forgiveness must go on to involve actual "transformation." The promise of "justification" in Romans 5 is followed by the call to "union" in Romans 6. "If there is no newness of life, no union with Christ, no coming out from under the dominion of sin, no yielding to the wooing of God's Spirit to come home to life in God's love,"[87] there is no fullness of salvation, no abundant Christian life.

The fullness is found in true relationship with Christ, in being immersed in God's love to the point of becoming its willing agent to a love-starved world. Against such love there is no law. As a result of such love, God's people discover themselves to be one family despite their diversity. In the face of such love, the world will take notice.

The Hesitation Must End

Holiness, the love-transformed new life in Christ, is a central theme and goal of biblical revelation. It's essential for the abundant Christian life and fundamental for understanding the history and future of the Church of God Movement. Even so, in recent generations the subject has been nearly silenced in the pulpits of the Movement. Reasons for this must be understood and the failure ended. Part of the problem involves inadequate definitions and failed metaphors. Needed now is a new language for an old and critical spiritual reality.

Ironically, while there is a current longing for holiness, there also is much hesitation surrounding it. Isn't the very idea of "holiness" basically archaic and elitist, an outdated Puritan ideal, a legalistic quagmire, a relic of medieval monasticism, a spiritual ideal not attainable? What is Christian holiness anyway?

We regularly hear variations of this stinging observation. "The church often doesn't encourage an inner life. It substitutes belief systems, belonging systems, and moral systems for interior journeys toward God. There is the Catholic hierarchy, Protestant Scripture interpretation, and fundamentalist mental gymnastics."[88] Despite the many challenges, true life in the Spirit, the holy life, is biblical and essential. Substitutes are unacceptable.

There are many questions and concerns, to be sure, but there also is the continuing biblical call to holiness. The Church of God Movement arose in the midst of the larger "Holiness Movement" of the late nineteenth century. The subject of holiness was addressed frequently in early Movement preaching and in its periodical, the *Gospel Trumpet*. By the 1950s, however, it was hardly on the Movement's center stage. Times had changed. The Movement still honored the idea of holiness, no doubt, but it was busy about other agendas. Long abandoned had been some old ideas about what holiness is and how it is to be received and lived.

This decline in emphasis must be reversed if the Movement is to be true to the call from the Bible that it claims to honor. The fact is that, as the whole Bible makes clear, the holy God has called a chosen people and intends this people be holy as God is holy.[89] Jesus expected his disciples to be holiness-hungry women and men, and accordingly he taught them the proper way to pray.

What's the "Lord's Prayer" all about? It's a guide for disciples who are longing for the right paths to seeking and being committed to the very things that God is and intends. We're instructed by the Lord to reverence God's holy name. In the process, it's promised that *we will be hallowed by God.*[90]

The holiness failures are there, of course, but so is the presence of the transforming grace of God. Preaching, teaching, and submitting to the demands of holiness aren't the easy ways for Christians to proceed in today's secular culture. However, they are the only ways forward if believers are to have integrity and be true representatives of Jesus because they have come to share his very image and mission. The yielding of our full personal identities is being demanded by God as the basis for receiving all that God is offering, which is nothing less than becoming *new creations in Christ.*

Holiness is more than radical personal renewal. It also remains the best—the only—bridge to realizing true Christian unity (see chapter nine). It's time to move on to concrete action that goes beyond constantly repeating idealistic rhetoric and criticizing the wrong ways of achieving unity. True unity will come only when the hearts of believers are melted together in the cleansing power of holiness sought, received, and lived out.

The Movement has believed the following from its beginning, and must not abandon it now. Holiness is the very nature of God. By God's sovereign choice, the holy, loving nature of God flows freely toward fallen humanity. Receiving it by faith and being transformed by it leads to Christ-likeness, the reflection of God's nature in humble disciples prepared to work for the reconciling of an unholy world.

Getting Beyond Mere Rhetoric

The need remains very real. God's people must come closer together for the sake of the great commission given by Jesus. Various paths to accomplishing unity were tried across the twentieth century, with some but limited success. The Church of God Movement for the most part has stayed on the sidelines of this "ecumenical" movement and had little impact on it churchwide. It kept up its vigorous holiness rhetoric while being less sure about what holiness is and exactly how it can implement Christian unity. A major history of the Movement is titled *The Quest for Holiness and Unity*.[91] This quest must continue and get more intentional, practical, and courageous.

The true tie among Christian believers, the only path to functional Christian unity, is the bond of divine love (holiness) provided by God's grace. The complicating fact is that even well-meaning believers bring to their corporate expressions of church life their varying personalities, preferences, language understandings, prejudices, and cultural backgrounds. Of course they do, and always will. These soon divide unless cleansed and constructively directed by deepening life in God's Spirit. When the cleansing comes, even though much of the diversity remains, the Spirit living within uses even the diversity for church enrichment rather causes of division.

How ironic that even the Holiness Movement, out of which the Church of God Movement emerged in the late nineteenth century, often failed in the unifying potential of Spirit-love and Spirit-cleansing. It became muddled in the quagmire of holiness legalisms and "hair-splitting." This distraction of personal and church trivia was fertile soil for the birth of small holiness-oriented denominations "that sometimes seemed more attentive to 'perfectionism' than to 'perfect love.' Rigidities emerged in a maze of theological nuances."[92]

That was the work of the enemy of the church and our souls. Daniel Warner was right. The dynamic of experienced holiness is the key to Christian unity, but it will overcome the many divisive tendencies only when separated from restrictive creeds and cumbersome structures that drag in destructive directions.

The Movement, sharply reacting to such unity failures, has intended far better for the whole church and its world witness. Even so, it now has experienced its own share of unity-blocking human distractions. Here are a few:

> How much adapting to common "holiness" dress standards should be tolerated?
>> (the big "necktie controversy" at the beginning of the twentieth century)
> How much emotion in worship is too much?
>> (resistance especially to the "tongues" emphasis of "Pentecostalism")
> How far do we dare "reach our hands in fellowship"?
>> (maybe not to believers who aren't in full accord with typical commitments of the Movement, avoiding guilt by association)
> Dare we move the North American Convention of the Church of God from its traditional location in Anderson, Indiana?
>> (a geographic tradition beloved by people committed to not allowing human tradition to control church life)
> Should ministerial candidates for ordination be approved if not making their examining colleagues theologically comfortable at all points?
>> (a common struggle with the creedal limits of non-creedalism)

These are only a few of the distracting points of tension experienced often by the Movement, threatening the unifying intent of "perfect love." It's hard to get beyond mere rhetoric and personal preferences and fears in order to make the holiness-to-unity ideal actually real. Nonetheless, the quest must go on for discovering the Spirit-enabled unity called for in the New Testament and strongly affirmed, at least in principle, by the Movement. Such unity, if achieved, will necessarily be both a gift of God *and* the hard work of God's people.

A first step is restoring a more biblical and practical understanding of Christian holiness for our time. A second is accepting the fact that God's gift of unity, possible only through a commonly shared new life in the Spirit, requires more than humbly accepting the transforming gift. It also requires active relationship building among sisters and brothers in the faith, establishing relationships that transcend church affiliations and variances in theological views and church practices and traditions. Unity must be *achieved*, not just gifted by God and discussed on occasion by God's people.

What is Christian "Holiness"?

Holiness is the most basic teaching of the entire Bible. God is presented as the ultimate holy One. God decided to create places and people undefiled and intended to be reflective of the character of the holy One. Things went wrong with the intruding presence of evil. The creation turned in on itself and has tried to exist for itself in defiance of God. It became tragically unholy.

In this awful circumstance, God acted lovingly to redeem the situation, eventually by sending the Son and Spirit as divine agents enabling a renewed holiness, a restored relationship to God and each other. Given this biblical background, holiness is hardly to be thought of as merely some rigid set of rules for perfect living. It is better defined as follows:

> Since believers are to be "holy as God is holy" (Lev. 11), holiness should be seen as *participation in the life of God*, a genuine change in human life made possible by acceptance of the offer of a restored divine-human relationship. Holiness is not a *thing* to be had or a *doctrine* to be formulated abstractly. It is the reality of God's character with which we are privileged by grace to relate transformingly. Believers are enabled to become *like* God as they relate to God in responding obedience—even though they never fully understand and certainly never control the divine.[93]

Instead of an impossible burden of life perfection for very imperfect people, Christian holiness should be thought of in more dynamic and exciting terms of a life possible for all sincere believers. Church of God Movement theologian Kenneth Jones put it well: "Holiness is an adventure because it means going through life *with* God. It's following our living Lord by his grace and help. It's walking by the moment-to-moment guidance of the Holy Spirit."[94] It's accepting the reign of God in our personal lives. It's becoming the light and love of Christ for others.

Holiness is our deliberate stance of openness to the Spirit of God so that the Spirit can help us become more like Jesus. In the simplicity of the Lord's Prayer, given by Jesus to holiness-hungry disciples, we are instructed "to bring the whole of our lives humbly before God so that God can begin to pour the richness of the Divine life into the whole of us."[95] This bringing and pouring, of course, doesn't cause us to become part of God, but it does grant us the privilege of being *God-indwelt*, and thus increasingly *God-like*.

Holiness is not to be thought of in discouragingly negative terms. Rather, it is "the ongoing invitation to host God's presence—a presence that radically transforms all our relationships. Sanctification is ultimately not *asceticism* (denying ourselves to death) or *athleticism* (working ourselves to death). Sanctification is *acceptance*—allowing God's Spirit to love us into new life, abundant life, and finally everlasting life."[96]

A helpful image of Christian holiness is a swimmer struggling to reach the water's surface in order to gulp life-sustaining air. Holiness is catching again God's breath, the necessity of real life. "Death is exhaled and the Spirit is inhaled deeply. Holiness is far less *something achieved* and much more *Someone received*."[97] Holiness is Christ coming within and his Spirit breathing new life, enabling Christ-likeness, applying the benefits of Christ's atoning work to our good and that of others.

Holiness is "letting go," exhaling death, taking ourselves off life's throne and "letting God." It's inhaling the divine life granted by pure grace, gladly placing God's sovereignty on our little life thrones. Suffocation is everywhere these days, but we are offered the wonder of an opportunity to catch the breath of life, the very life of the Eternal! "Then the Lord formed humans from the dust of the ground and breathed into their nostrils the breath of life" (Gen. 2:7). It can be now as it was in the beginning, transformed from dust to life.

When a person lets go and lets God, that person is given a gift, new life and membership in the family of the redeemed and transformed. This family is then called to be a representative agent of Christ in this world. There comes by grace an increased oneness in the Spirit that propels the "saints" into common engagement with God's ongoing life and life-giving mission.

There are two rather distinct phases of the spiritual journey with Jesus—although they can be experienced differently and must not be strictly formularized. The first is about getting to know Jesus in his forgiving grace, and the second is about the choice to follow Jesus to a personal cross and new-life resurrection. First, we accept who Jesus really is and take advantage of his readiness to erase our wayward past. Then we are invited to look to the future and allow the Spirit of Jesus to re-shape who we now are and how we now will live as part of the ongoing Jesus mission.

From God's Mountain-top to the World's Valleys

Jesus is to be our Savior and then also our Lord. Holiness is involved in each of these and only fulfilled in the realization of both.

Choosing new life in the Spirit of Jesus, phase two of the spiritual journey, is Christian "holiness." First-phase, half-way Christians may make it to heaven but they aren't likely to do much changing of the needs of today's churches and world. If we're to be whole, full-phase Christians, we must experience forgiving love and then determine to become agents of that love by making Jesus the Lord of our future lives at any cost, even a cross.

Christian holiness is accepting God's will as our own. It's the full spiritual journey of forgiveness and life re-creation, of illumination on the mountain and dedication to ministry in the valleys below. Daniel Warner, the Movement's primary pioneer, was right in focusing on the cruciality of Christian holiness. His major book was *Bible Proofs of the Second Work of Grace* (1880). It pointed straight to a central truth of all biblical revelation.

I recognize that Warner was overly wooden and legalistic in his handling of some biblical texts, and even wrong in his "eradication" theory of sanctification.[98] I offer no defense of such things. He was very right, however, at least about this. The full Christian experience is God's expectation of and provision for us sinful humans. The fullness involves being with Jesus on the mountain-top of forgiveness and then, as changed and empowered persons, willingly with him in his world mission in the troubled valleys below.

The intended fullness of Christian experience involves both receiving forgiveness and then experiencing increasing stages of actual new creation in Christ. This new creation is designed to spread the overflow of divine grace and love to all the crying needs of the world. "Holiness" for the Christian is "the whole person redirected towards the highest spiritual end, likeness to Christ."[99] The heart of its meaning is captured well in these lyrics by a Movement's beloved composer:

> More like Christ, my heart is praying,
> More like Christ from day to day,
> All his graces rich displaying,
> While I tread my pilgrim way.[100]

The two-phased grace journey to wholeness in Christ and increasingly reflective of Christ forms a natural bridge. It provides the way for the individual believer to to Christian unity among believers, regardless of church affiliation. Being immersed in the life-changing and love-rich grace of God inspires and enables those so immersed to join hands and reach out to share God's amazing love with others. More maturity in Christian experience leads to more effective Christian mission in the world.

NEEDED CONVERSATION AND ACTION

1. How would you define "holiness"? Where in the Bible are we informed about what Christian holiness really is and why it's so important?

2. Do you believe that biblical holiness is relevant to the twenty-first century? Recall that, in the Movement's teaching tradition, holiness was very important initially, became less emphasized over the generations, and now is urgently needed again.

3. What particular statements in this chapter do you think best describe Christian holiness and its significance for Christian life and witness today? Are there statements that you are struggling with? Where might you go to get the needed help? Are you willing to accept the high personal cost, leaving your self-centeredness and becoming Christ-like?

4. Why do you think that holiness has been a major theme, theological belief, and foundational basis for the Church of God Movement and many other faith groups? Why do you think that some Christian faith groups do not embrace a holiness tradition?

5. How has the "misinterpretation" or the "abuse" of the teaching of holiness impacted how some view the church? Has poor theology about holiness impacted you personally or your family, keeping you away from what is central to Christian believing and living?

6. In the congregation you attend, have you heard many sermons recently on Christian holiness? If not, why do you think that is?

7. As a clearly imperfect person, does becoming "perfect in love" seem like an impossible life goal? Would God expect of us what is impossible?

THE MEANING OF
SANCTIFICATION

CHARLES E. BROWN
FOREWORD BY BARRY L. CALLEN

A comprehensive history of the
Church of God Reformation Movement

THE QUEST
for Holiness & Unity
Second Edition

By John W. V. Smith

Revised & Expanded by
Merle D. Strege

Chapter 9

HOLINESS: BRIDGE TO CHRISTIAN UNITY

Christian holiness is a divine love received that then is to be allowed to actively reach, relate, heal, and reconcile. It inspires a "catholic spirit" among believers that builds bridges instead of walls. It's God's "Gulf Stream" that warms the cold ocean through which it flows. How sweet this bond of "perfectness"!

Wholeness of life in God's grace is the abundance of Christian holiness. It's a magnificent and progressive possibility, and also the vital link between the spiritual renewal of individual believers and the great need for Christian unity in the church.

The needed unity among Christians, long envisioned and proclaimed by the Church of God Movement, certainly isn't that one day all Christians will come under one master church organization or gladly affirm one master creedal statement. Rather, it's what the Movement's beloved R. Eugene Sterner once said:

> Our dream is to proclaim and practice the will of God as revealed in Jesus Christ and unfolded in the dynamic relationships in the first-century church. It's not to become sectarian but to stand open on the God-ward side to learn all the truth we can know and be open on the man-ward side to loving fellowship with all our Christian brothers and sisters. The Church of God should be a movement, a catalytic fellowship and leavening influence lifting up the essential nature of Christian unity, namely a unity in the person, power, and love of Christ.[101]

There's the dream lying at the very heart of the Movement. Rooted in biblical revelation and affirmed by the witness of the apostolic church, believers in Christ are to be open to personal cleansing by God and thus increasingly be open to relating actively to all who are experiencing that grace-enabled cleansing. This openness and mutual experiencing becomes the natural bridge to common mission propelled by the one unifying Spirit.

Mutual Slavery in Christ

We read in Galatians 5 that "for freedom Christ has set us free. Stand firm, therefore, and do not submit again to a yoke of slavery. You were called to freedom, brothers and sisters; only do not use your freedom as an opportunity for self-indulgence, but through love become slaves to one another." Yes, believers are to be *slaves to one other*.

The vision of the Movement is one of a wonderful, mutual slavery in the freedom of God's liberating grace. It's the vision of the church not being a center of human religious machinery but a Spirit-filled family bound together and serving together by the energy of the love of God showered on all by God's sanctifying Spirit.

The family of God is the fellowship of all who are new creations in Christ. The spiritually reborn are united because of their common sharing in the same life-giving breath of God who is renewing their lives and binding them together in love. Note these beloved words of a 1893 song by Daniel Warner, primary pioneer of the Movement. The word "perfectness" refers to holiness, the unifying bond of God's cleansing love:

> How sweet this bond of perfectness,
> The wondrous love of Jesus;
> A pure foretaste of heaven's bliss,
> Oh, fellowship so precious!

> *Refrain:*
> Oh, beloved, how this perfect love
> Unites us all in Jesus!
> One heart, and soul, and mind we prove
> The union heaven gave us.

> Oh, praise the Lord for love divine
> That binds us all together;
> Our souls in fellowship embrace,
> And live in sweet communion.

Holiness is divine love received, a love that then begins actively reaching, building, bridging, and unifying. It's an embracing fellowship living in sweet communion.

The beloved Samuel G. Hines, native of Jamaica and longtime Movement pastor in the United States, was a leader in the demanding task of reconciliation, racial and otherwise. He was fond of saying, "The Church of God deserves an 'A' for its message of unity, but an 'F' for its practice." Even if that judgment is a bit severe, it's generally well-founded. Cheryl Sanders, Curtiss DeYoung, and others in the Movement were inspired by Hines and his close colleague James Earl Massey to carry forward the struggle for Christian reconciliation.[102]

Now is the time for followers of Christ to get on with the hard work of making real the unity ideal. Progress will always be partial, yes, but that's no excuse for not proceeding with what's possible. An old saying is pertinent. One can count the seeds in an apple, but one cannot begin to count the potential number of apples in a seed. So, plant! Plant unity seeds even when the fruit may be harvested only by generations still to come.

Experienced and expressed holiness is the key. It inspires a "catholic spirit" that dislikes walls. Rather, it builds networks of loving and serving relationships intended to involve the whole church as it reaches as one toward the whole globe.

The "Catholic Spirit"

Holiness is being infused and renewed and commissioned by the re-creating love and grace of God. To be holy is a community-creating force. A significant part of the historic roots of the Church of God Movement has been the Wesleyan revival beginning in the eighteenth century. A prominent aspect of the teaching of John Wesley was what he called the "catholic spirit."

In a sermon by that title, Wesley used 2 Kings 10:15 and its image of two hearts each being made right with God and thus each being prepared to take the hand of the other in common fellowship and service.

He spells out what is meant by a "right heart." It's the heart made "right with God and filled with the energy of love."

And what does this rightness, filled with the energy of love, imply about relationships with fellow believers of any church affiliation? Wesley concluded, as later the Church of God Movement would, that there should be an "unspeakable tenderness" that causes one to lay down life itself for the sake of the beloved sister or brother in Christ.

Reflecting Wesley, T. Franklin Miller, prominent Movement leader, would put it this way. "The dream that I hope will possess us [the Movement] is that we might demonstrate the unity of believers and bear witness to the truth wherever found, leavening Christendom with the simple and full message of the New Testament. We must reach our hands in fellowship. While we work at removing barriers and building bridges, the Holy Spirit will work the miracle of spiritual unity."[103]

This spiritual unity has the power and will to build bridges that connect believers. Common life in the Spirit is unity's seedbed. The resulting responsibility for Spirit-filled believers is to plant in that fertile ground, removing barriers to the free flow of Christian fellowship and service. The essence of Christian holiness leads to its intended fruit, the "catholic spirit," the spiritual instinct to be a whole community of disciples of the one Master.

Beginnings of Bridge Work

The Church of God Movement for too long has sought safety in being absent from the bridge-building action going on in the larger Christian community. It's been announcing the ideal of Christian unity from the sidelines. If it's to serve the larger church as it hopes, helping to reform it truly by activating the God-given unity potential, the Movement must dare to be seen and known where the unifying action is.

Let's finally hear well the Movement's beloved James Earl Massey. "True reformation is accomplished from within, not from beyond the rest of the church. Vital contact is our need. It remains for us to raise the curtain of exclusivity behind which we have done our living and let the rest of the church world see us—not as a group set apart but as a people concerned about the rest of the church and open to other church bodies."[104]

For too long Movement leaders have practiced "exclusivity" by rarely being active in the "ecumenical movement" or at first even in local ministerial associations. The latter has largely changed, and in a very few cases even the former. Gilbert W. Stafford, from his base in the Movement's seminary in Anderson, Indiana, associated actively and productively with the Faith and Order Commission of the National Council of Churches (U.S.A.) and wrote of the significant benefits given and received by being there.[105] Certain of his successors in the seminary have continued this participation.

Anderson School of Theology in 1984 hosted a conference on the "Concept of the Believers Church," followed in 1999 by my extensive published presentation of the history and theology of the Believers Church tradition in Christianity.[106] T. Franklin Miller led the Movement's Board of Christian Education and later Warner Press in being partners in the "Committee on the Uniform Series" of the National Council of Churches. That curriculum continues as the "Bridges" program of the Movement. Otto F. Linn was part of a committee of the National Council of Churches working on the original *Revised Standard* translation of the Bible.

Kimberly Majeski of Anderson School of Theology and Christian Ministries currently serves as chair of a program unit of the Wesleyan Theological Society. Now Dean Emeritus of that seminary, Barry L. Callen functioned as Editor of the *Wesleyan Theological Journal* for over twenty years and now, representing the Movement, functions as Editor of Aldersgate Press of the inter-denominational Wesleyan Holiness Connection.

The WHC is seeking actively to reignite awareness of the significance of Christian holiness for the renewal of today's Wesleyan-related denominations.[107] It's a movement, much like the Church of God Movement, calling for the wholeness of Christian experience (holiness) and the possibility of a resulting wholeness of the church (unity). The WHC's web address, so reflective of the goals of the Movement, is *holinessandunity.org*.

David Lawson, Gilbert Stafford, Keith Huttenlocker, Barry Callen, and others led a decade-long dialogue among leaders of the Movement and those of the Independent Christian Churches/Churches of Christ. This process in the 1980s and 1990s resulted in the book *Coming Together in Christ* co-authored by James North and Barry Callen. Sub-titled "Pioneering a New Testament Way to Christian Unity," it chronicles the journey of these two bodies, both committed to Christian unity and finally attempting active bridge-building to each other.

The working premise of this ten-year dialogue was: "We as Christians will be more the church that we ought to be, and reach more effectively in mission as it ought to be, *only* as we work at being together in Christ and enabled for service by the power of the Spirit of Christ."[108] The dialogue was never about "merger" but all about "mission." It yielded some good unifying fruit, but mostly only for those directly involved. The larger constituencies of the two bodies were informed of the progress, but for the most part they remained absorbed in their usual agendas.

James Earl Massey appeared in the pulpits of numerous denominational seminaries, universities, and conventions. He was the pride of the Movement who became known as the "Prince of Preachers" of the late twentieth and early twenty-first centuries.[109]

Robert Pearson, former General Director of Church of God Ministries, established Horizon International in 2001, gathering a range of denominations in the United States and several African nations around an urgent mission to AIDS orphans. Barry Callen has served as Horizon's corporate secretary since the organization's beginning.

Curtiss DeYoung currently serves as the chief executive officer of the Minnesota Council of Churches and is widely recognized for his publications in Christian "reconciliation" studies. Susie Cunningham Stanley was key to the formation of the Wesleyan Women Clergy organization. These Movement individuals were remarkable bridge-builders, but they have been too few, and such efforts have been too isolated from the mainstream of Movement life.

"Christian Churches Together" is one of the more significant of today's Christian ecumenical bodies, comprised of a range of church "families." James Lyon, present General Director of Church of God Ministries, serves as a member of CCT's Steering Committee and is the occasional voice for the Evangelical/Pentecostal family. He advocates for ministry relationships beyond the borders of church affiliations.

The 2019 General Assembly of the Movement in the United States and Canada featured a partnership with Christian bodies like CDF Capital and Brotherhood Mutual. Meanwhile, Servant Solutions of the Movement, led capably by Jeff Jenness and now Jim O'Bold, was serving the clergy of several denominational bodies with quality financial planning and other retirement needs. The Movement's slogan, "we reach our hands in fellowship to every blood-washed one," was finding some practical traction. It's done so regularly through the many institutional and military chaplains of the Movement and through its numerous missionaries who have been ministering cross-culturally around the world for many generations.[110]

These are examples of the trans-denominational bridge builders of the Church of God Movement. Miller, Hines, Stafford, Massey, Callen, Pearson, Lawson, DeYoung, Stanley, Majeski, Lyon, Jenness, and O'Bold are some of the inspired movers beyond mere holiness-unity rhetoric. They have been visible, practical, and significant beginnings of the desired future for the widening ministries of the Movement. Many more inspired movers are urgently needed.

Such Movement leaders have actively joined holiness, unity, and church mission by linking the hands and hearts of Christian brothers and sisters church-wide in the life and cause of Christ. They have understood these twin Christian truths:

> *Truth one*: Christian unity is a gift of God's grace, so that every Christian belongs to all other Christians as a spiritual birthright.
>
> *Truth two*: the gift of unity must be *gained* by intentional bridging actions. The birthright must be activated. As the 1974 Yokefellow Statement of the Movement says, "We encourage through every means possible the establishing and maintaining of work relationships with other like-minded groups on the national, state, and local levels."

An ecumenical church leader once addressed the Movement's General Assembly. He was clearly appreciative of the Movement's emphasis on Christian unity, saying that "it is a message we all need to hear expounded and demonstrated." Billy Melvin, Director of the National Association of Evangelicals, then stated his concern pointedly. "Why have I not seen more involvement of the Church of God Movement in the organization I represent? I believe you have something to share with those larger bodies of Christ." One thing to share, he said, is "your beautiful job of involving our Black brothers and sisters and other ethnics and minorities in your fellowship."

Whatever insight, accomplishment, or resource a Christian community has, it is obligated to share it with other Christian communities, and also receive enrichment from the responding sharing of others. To be holy means, among other things, desiring wholeness of understanding and unity of mission engagement. It's having and activating the "catholic spirit."

Why has the Movement not been more active in building the bridges espoused from its beginning? One answer is that the Movement has been too absorbed in its own evolving life, quietly adding to the division it has critiqued so vigorously. Another answer is that it has judged the uniting efforts of others to be false approaches to Christian, approaches with which the Movement hasn't want to be associated. It's now time for the Movement to get more outside itself, outside its fear, and beyond its historic preoccupation with critiquing others.

God's Gulf Stream

Images are helpful in thinking about complex realities. A Christian renewal movement's relationship to the larger church is complex and may be pictured this way. The Gulf Stream is a marvelous movement of water. It flows as a river of warmth from the Gulf of Mexico across the Atlantic Ocean all the way to portions of Europe. Its general path can be mapped and its influence measured. Its exact boundaries, however, are imprecise. It's always open to all the surrounding ocean, influencing and being influenced as it moves along.

The opposite image would be that of a sealed pipeline stretching across the ocean. This would be a highly controlled movement of water neither warming nor being enriched by the surrounding ocean as its sealed internal flow moves along. The Church of God Movement has sought to be a stream, an enriching and enriched flowing of the water of life, a *movement* and not a self-contained and self-absorbed pipeline (denominational*ism*). Renewal movements within the church's life, like the Church of God Movement, should be a living organism that's not preoccupied with themselves but with the needs of the church as a whole. They should strive to warm the whole church toward increased wholeness and mission effectiveness.

A Commission of Christian Unity was launched by the Movement in 1965, intended to facilitate the Movement's cooperative work among Christians by making contacts, holding conversations, and developing lines of mission cooperation. All of the Movement's previous standing commissions were dissolved in the 1990s when Church of God Ministries was formed. The intent was not to end positive outreaches, but little seems to get accomplished unless there is a structure dedicated to a particular task.

The reaching now needed in the Movement is not only to other Christian faith communities but also to elements of its own constituency. Currently being envisioned by Church of God Ministries is increased communication with and cooperation among diverse assemblies of the Movement world-wide. There is no effective standing venue to facilitate such cooperation initiative. The Movement is allergic to structures, while wishing the results that structures alone seem able to bring. Bridges don't get built without supporting infrastructures. The Movement now needs an international venue to help end its own considerable fragmentation.

Because church bodies, even unity movements, have a tendency toward self-preoccupation, we now turn to a difficult question. How does a reform movement within the church, one existing for the sake of the greater unity of the church, avoid adding to the church's division by its own very existence? How does an *organism organize* without threatening the integrity of its own life?

NEEDED CONVERSATION AND ACTION

1. If the needed unity among Christians, long envisioned and proclaimed by the Church of God Movement, isn't that one day all Christians will come under one master church organization or gladly affirm one master creedal statement, then what is it?

2. Much in the early phase of the Movement's life involved "coming out" and arguing against other believers thought to have gone wrong in their theological understandings and organized church life. Does a commonly experienced Christian holiness dissolve the walls separating believers and transform relationships through a unifying love?

3. Are you willing to test the enriching and unifying process of thinking carefully with instead of over against Christian brothers and sisters of traditions other than your own? Such an extended conversation among major Christian thinkers is provided by Barry L. Callen. It features the active participation of Movement leaders James Earl Massey

and Barry L. Callen. See Heart of the Matter: Frank Conversations among Great Christian Thinkers on the Major Subjects of Christian Theology (Emeth Press, rev. ed., 2016). The church, to be its best self, must be a community of ongoing conversation that is frank and up-building.

4. What does the New Testament mean by a "mutual slavery" among believers? Are you prepared to begin the selfless "bridge work" called for? Believers who have experienced the "abundant life" are to work toward the wholeness and mission effectiveness of the whole church together.

5. The Movement has historic roots in the Wesleyan theological tradition. That includes having the "catholic spirit." What is that and are you filled with it?

6. Images are important for picturing complex truths. One important image is the church flowing through the world as a "Gulf Stream." What exactly does that mean?

7. Who is responsible for creating an environment for and commitment to building relational bridges among believers? Is it national or state church leaders, the pastors, or maybe you?

TRYING TO ORGANIZE AN ORGANISM

Because the church is understood to be a divine organism, the living family of believers, there is understandable reluctance in the Church of God Movement to create structures that might develop lives of their own at odds with the church's very nature and mission. Nonetheless, "A great theology, clearly understood, and great overarching goals, clearly conceived, mean little in themselves unless they are carefully harnessed to help the church and its people carry forward significant ministry. The need now is for an increasingly adequate *structure* to serve as a channel for implementing the mission."[111]

The church is a family of believers, a living organism, a current expression of the active ministry of God's Spirit. Mere humans cannot constitute, contain, control, or organize this living, divine reality. What they can and should do, however, is be good stewards of the work and mission of the church to which they belong and are called to represent by God's grace. The church is a divine-human reality. This paradox has long troubled the Church of God Movement. Its leaders who seek effective administration of the church's life are caught between contrasting realities.[112]

The Movement has been committed strongly to understanding the church as the family of God, constituted and controlled by God's Spirit. The biography of the Movement's primary pioneer, Daniel S. Warner, is understandably titled *It's God's Church!* Indeed it is. Nonetheless, God's church is also our common responsibility as members of God's family, not to constitute or control, but to activate and coordinate the body's life and mission.

The Movement suffers from a lack of will to be proactive in functioning together in organized ways. It's leaned heavily on the divine side of the paradox. Its Movement's 1963 All-Boards Congress admitted that "the need now is for an increasingly adequate *structure* to serve as a channel for implementing the mission." That may be the reported need, but there continues to be strong resistance to any such structure actually emerging.

Anything that smacks of "top down" decision-making faces hard times.[113] New ministries emerge around the edges of the Movement, tending to further fragment its life. This Movement so committed to Christian unity now must come to terms with its own tendency to internal dis-unity. The paradox needs some re-balancing.

Structures in Support of Mission

Structure is always necessary for the stability and sustainability of any community, even the community of Christian believers. God's church is indeed a living organism of the Spirit, constituted, gifted, and sent by God. Nonetheless, the members of God's chosen body are to be faithful stewards of God's mission in this world.

An immediate caution is appropriate, of course. Organization in support of church mission always should be developed and maintained in light of a central biblical truth. Commissioned at Pentecost was the *koinonia*, the "fellowship of the Spirit" (Acts 2:42). This koinonia is the living *organism* out of which and in light of which the organizations of the church should emerge and always be judged.

The Movement exists in part to remind all church bodies—and now itself—that "where you have the koinonia you have the church; where you do not have the koinonia, you have a religious organization, but not the church, except in name."[114] Given this core fact, one question has troubled and hampered the Movement from its beginning. How does one *organize* an *organism* without destroying the free-flowing existence of the living thing?

The Movement has understood itself to be only a *movement*, an interim body, not a fixed denomination. As such, how does an interim non-organization organize to accomplish its reforming task and spread its needed insights without deteriorating into another fixed church institution within the already divided church? Movement leaders eventually answered in part with the justification that they were attempting to organize the *work* of the church, never the *church itself*.

A struggle the Movement always has faced is the difficult clash between *autonomy* and *authority* in church life. These are twin commitments of the Movement, although they seem at odds with each other. From almost the Movement's beginning, they have seemed equally legitimate and necessary. It's a dilemma that's never been resolved. Believers are truly free in Christ, and yet they also are truly bound to each other. How can this bond be translated into the will to work together in an intentionally coordinated way?

Trustees were required legally for a local church to own property, so trustees reluctantly began to be named soon after the Movement began. Formal church authorization was required for clergy to qualify for railroad passes, so authorization was given in 1902, again reluctantly. Independent mission enterprises in the Movement's life abroad soon were getting chaotic. So, with caution but a sense of necessity, the ministers formed a "Missionary Committee" in 1909 to bring some order—hopefully without restricting the work of the Spirit.

In 1917 a little college was founded in Anderson, Indiana, now Anderson University, and in 1918 the also new General Ministerial Assembly quickly acted to accept this modest new educational reality, but only with a formal caution. It said that human intellectual study must never be allowed to supplant divine gifting for ministry. This caution still persists even though the Movement's current four universities in the United States function without the 1918 restriction. Serious preparation for ministerial ordination is valued and expected, but without any particular formal education required. This leaves the Movement's seminary in Anderson, Indiana, in an awkward and weak position, trapped in the ongoing paradox.

The persisting problem is still the stubborn and overly controlling presence of *autonomy* in the Movement's life. One prominent consultant for this book put it bluntly. "I recommend that you give autonomy a bloody nose and a black eye!" Ronald Duncan, previous General Director of Church of God Ministries, called it "a cancer" in the Movement's present life and wrote a "white paper" on the subject that is still being read by ordination candidates in the Leadership Focus program.

A beloved missionary once stated the Movement's overriding vision: "It is our avowed purpose to become no more than a spiritual movement within the divided church: (1) teaching and living the central truths of the New Testament; (2) endeavoring to keep the unity of the Spirit in the bond of peace (Eph. 4); (3) holding to Christ as the supreme head of the church; and (4) not professing to have all the answers but believing that there is enough known truth that, if obeyed, could unite God's people and save a lost world."[115]

The resulting dilemma of this wonderful vision has been how best to proceed. How can the Movement work to unite God's people and save a lost world without developing functional ministry structures through which the work can get done? How does a "movement" organize a living organism without strangling the fluidity of its life in the process?

The Movement's answer to the organizational dilemma has been to develop cooperative tools and seek voluntary participation. Structures that are created must be tentative, limiting the chance of their developing lives of their own. Leadership of the structures must be held strictly accountable for not leading beyond what the diverse body of volunteers is ready to tolerate. In fact, to the surprise of many outside the Movement, this approach has worked relatively well. Much amazing ministry has been accomplished despite the significant strictures of group diversity and complete volunteerism.

The concept of complete volunteerism has deep roots in the Church of God Movement, roots that appear to go deeper than those found in the Bible, where "covenant" and "community" and mutual responsibility to the faith community are basic. Consequently, calls for intentional togetherness are gaining ground in today's Movement, despite strong resistance. The witness of Dr. Ronald Duncan, former General Director of Church of God Ministries, is a prime example. Since 2013 he has been the Executive Director of the Global Wesleyan Alliance, and now reports:

> These "Holiness Groups" [comprising the Alliance] are getting the job done because they can spend their time on mission rather than on wrangling about structure and who is in charge. Are their denominational systems perfect? No, yet they are fulfilling Matthew 28:19-20 better than the Church of God Movement is. I am convinced that many leaders of our Movement need to go to the desert (Gal. 1:13-17) to allow God to reorient their thinking so that God can have the preeminence.[116]

Has the anti-structure bias become more the egos of local leaders than the actual biblical mandate? This is a provocative question few are ready to address openly.

Patterns of Church Organization

If structure is needed for effective church life, what guidance is given in the New Testament for how to go about this organizing task?

The New Testament presents no pre-set blueprint for the proper organization of the church's life. It's to be motivated instead by what disciples understand to be *the main thing*, the evangelistic mission of the church (see detail in chapter eleven). The Bible presents a range of undeveloped and experimental answers to the organizational question. The earliest attempts at forming the church's structure appear to have been local or regional efforts to discover in differing circumstances the best ways of promoting the main thing, accomplishing the church's core mission.

The Bible focuses on goal and function, not form. Jesus came with a message of the arriving kingdom of God, not one of any planned religious establishment. The emerging church seen in the New Testament "was not in search of a perfect organization as an end in itself; instead, it was devoted to the spread of the gospel, to maturation in the life of Christ, and to the development of a unified witness to the world."[117] There's the main thing! The "how" remained an open question.

We see in the New Testament three general patterns for the possible organizing of the church's life on behalf of its mission. None are fully developed or set forth as mandatory for how God's children are to live and work together in all times and places. Each is a way of trying to serve the main thing in the best way available, always featuring the Spirit's freedom, enablement, and guidance.

Over time, each of these three embryonic "apostolic" patterns would be fully developed and institutionalized by one or many bodies of Christian believers. Sometimes each has been claimed to be the only way for all Christians to structure their community and ministry activities. Organizations, including church organizations, often gain lives of their own and mirror the "worldly" organizations around them. In a few centuries after the New Testament events, much of the church became organized on the hierarchical system of the Roman Empire. Unfortunately, strong political forces had greatly influenced the church's life.

The Church of God Movement has resisted vigorously this hierarchical tendency, opting for the opposite, "congregationalism," as the best way to go, even the only acceptable organizational way. It's been presumed that full control of church life at the local level is the proper organizational pattern for responding to New Testament directives. Even so, choosing any organizational option for the church, including congregationalism, and then institutionalizing it in a mandatory manner, is to risk laying human hands too heavily on God's church.

Organizing the life of the church in any rigid manner threatens the very life of the church. Insisting that the Spirit of God wishes to minister through only one organizational pattern, or no pattern, is projecting backwards on the New Testament a "revelation" that isn't there. It tends to block the free flow of the ministry of the Spirit among believers as they journey and seek to serve relevantly together in diverse and fluid circumstances.

The Movement has seen this danger clearly and wished very much to be "apostolic" in message and approach. Unfortunately, it has restricted its life unnecessarily by its excessive fear of any organization and authority being established beyond the local level. It's had difficulty learning the following lesson.

Avoiding the risks of church organization by denying the legitimacy of any organization, or by insisting on only one pattern of organization, can also be hurtful to the church's central mission. Too little organization tends to encourage chaos. While sometimes claiming that an organizational vacuum is more open to the Spirit's freedom than any formalized structure, the Movement has struggled to realize that such unstructured openness is highly vulnerable to a range of contrary spirits.

Here as elsewhere, the Church of God Movement should benefit more than it has from its Wesleyan heritage. John Wesley saw clearly in his revival the vital link between spiritual experience and disciplined structures. Structures are legitimate, even necessary, when they are designed to nurture and employ Christian experience on behalf of the church's mission. Wesley's "system of societies, classes, and bands in large measure formed the genius of the discipline, growth, and enduring impact of Methodism."[118] The Movement would benefit from more of such a "system."

Three general organizational patterns are seen in embryo form in the New Testament. They are the episcopal, presbyterian, and congregational models. They differ mostly in where decision-making authority is judged to belong best. The first sees authority residing in select apostolic leaders whose right to leadership comes directly from God and is handed down from the first apostles to select clergy successors. The second broadens the leadership base to inter-congregational assemblies of church leaders often elected in a democratic way on the basis of perceived leadership gifts. The third focuses church leadership in local congregations not answerable to anyone beyond themselves.

Time has shown that each of these patterns of church life can serve well the church's mission, and each also can fossilize into a self-serving mission distraction. Christians often ask which of the three patterns is most appropriate, most biblical, most intended by the Lord? The answer will not please some. It is, "all and none of them."

The Movement today should choose wisely what organizational questions it judges most important. They should *not* be these:

- Which of us has found in the New Testament the truly biblical form of church organization? There is none to be found.

- How has the Movement handled the church organization question—shouldn't that be our future guide? There's been growth in understanding and numerous false starts not necessarily worth repeating.

- Shouldn't we avoid creating any structures that might make us look like a "denomination"? This fear should not be allowed to keep blocking what serves best the work of the Spirit in our time and settings.

Here are perennial questions that today's Movement must address creatively and courageously.

- If we must organize the church's work to be responsible servants of the church's mission, and we must, then how can we best further the church's mission today without strangling the organism of the Spirit?

- How can the church, in its current circumstances, best mobilize its personnel and resources to most effectively accomplish God's work in the world?

- How can we overcome our great fear of being "denominational" so that we don't predetermine answers to the above questions before they are carefully considered?

The church always should be prepared to heed the Spirit's voice as Christ's missional wind blows. Thus, church organization, whatever its form, should be flexible and mission focused. The model of church structure must encourage the New Testament call to the unity of disciples, featuring an inter-connectedness of the whole church as much as possible. There must be more of a reaching of hands than a building of high walls that divide believers and weaken their common mission efforts.

The Spirit of Jesus is the Heart and Guide of the church. Jesus is the central Subject. The structures and strategies of the church's ministries must be adjusted as times change and the Spirit of God moves in the changes. However the church structures its life together, the goal must be allowing the wind of the Spirit to blow freely through its members on behalf of the church's mission.

A Reluctant Pattern Emerges

The Church of God Movement was a burst of nineteenth-century reforming idealism about the church as she ought to be, purified and functioning outside denominational compromises and divisions. In a very few generations, however, there came the realization that one cannot reach the top of God's intended mountain simply by looking up with the eyes and extolling its beauty with the lips. There also must be intentionality, specific initiatives, and even church structures and empowered leadership thoughtfully designed and carefully authorized.

The local congregations of the Movement soon were forced toward some formal organization in order to own property and function in a highly organized society. By 1917 there was the organization of the General Ministerial Assembly (United States and Canada). Its evolving life and actions over the decades have been chronicled in the reference work *Leaning Forward!* (2019). This General Assembly, as it's now known, has sought to lead as possible without having any "ecclesiastical authority."

Beginning in the 1920s, a series of ministry agencies emerged, joining the publishing company to focus on the needs for Christian education, church extension, and missionary work. These agencies led relatively independent lives that finally were combined into "Church of God Ministries" as the twenty-first century opened. This merging of ministries into one entity was an intentional effort at increasing efficiency and lessening the organizational fragmentation that had evolved over the decades.

Beginning in the 1930s, a series of state/regional/provincial assemblies came into existence across the Movement in the United States and Canada. Considerable ministry activity beyond the local congregational level soon was lodged in these free-standing organizations. Their legal relationship to the General Assembly was not clearly defined until 2017 when the General Assembly assumed full control of the Movement's ministerial credentialing. This was judged necessary in part because allowing wide variance in standards and procedures was unfair and unacceptable given the growing legal threats to ministers and congregations. Beyond credentialing, however, legal relationships and accountabilities still remain unclear.

The authorized *Credentials Manual* now makes clear for the first time that the General Assembly is exercising actual authority, but only in the arena of ministerial credentialing. Other relationships remain undefined. Area assemblies associated with the General Assembly continue to function independently, with legal questions unresolved. "Project Imagine" worked for two years (2017-2018) to find some increased clarity and efficiency in this fragmented circumstance, but with limited progress made. See detail below.

Beyond Israel's Error

In all of these organizational developments in the Movement over the decades, there has been a tendency toward some modest "centralization" because of perceived necessity. In reaction, there always has been resistance because of the Movement's strong loyalty to the value of freedom from the dangers of wayward church structures. Of what is the Movement constantly afraid? It's afraid of deteriorating like ancient Israel when it wanted to be "like the nations." The fear is becoming "just another denomination."

Two competing viewpoints existed in ancient Israel. Some Jews were calling for a monarchy like their neighbors, a seeming practical necessity if they were to survive as a divinely called people in this troubled world. Others insisted that such a kingly development would be a serious error, a disastrous compromise since God should be their only king. The Church of God Movement has chosen to avoid all monarchy-like establishments.

Long experience suggests, however, that there are more than the two alternatives. In the face of considerable organizational inefficiency, duplication of effort, lack of cooperation and communication, and sometimes even uncoordinated confusion in the Movement's life, surely God would be pleased with some thoughtful "works" to join an idealistic faith. Salvation is by faith alone, yes, but saving faith should never be alone. With it should come the thoughtful works of a planned stewardship of resources, opportunities, and obligations.

Every community, including the church, needs vision and structure, the dynamic of forward expectation and the foothold of experienced tradition that together provide order to its life. The pioneers of the Movement were challenging excessive and suffocating order, humanly devised and heavily controlled church structures seen as strangling the free flow of the Spirit of God. Time has shown that these pioneers reacted understandably, but overreacted when calling for all human hands to be taken off the church's functioning. Some practicality needs to prevail for vision to become functional reality.

The Movement's own principle of proper church order has placed priority on the liberating, empowering, and commissioning ministry of God's Spirit, the only rightful One to order the church's life. Even so, "structure" appeared quickly in the Movement's life. Daniel Warner may have been the original visionary and primary energizer of the Movement but, following his death in 1895, E. E. Byrum quickly brought order, form, and cohesion to a young Movement that otherwise might have splintered and even ceased to exist. When he stepped down as Editor of the *Gospel Trumpet* in 1916, Byrum had wielded pervasive influence in the life of the Movement.

The tension of human-Divine partnership in church life is real and difficult. On the one hand, Movement pioneers were right. God wills that the church be unencumbered by self-serving human institutionalism. On the other hand, church members must organize the work of God without acting like they've imprisoned God in their belief statements and church structures.

The concern for today's Movement is twofold. The visionary fire of Daniel Warner must never be supplanted by the paralyzing fumes of endless church bureaucracy. Nor must that fire be allowed to be only theoretical rhetoric lacking the structured ability to actually impact church life and mission today. An organizational lesson learned from the Movement's struggling past must be factored into current church structuring and ministry strategizing.

Here's the lesson. The fear of establishing structured authority opens the church to unnecessary waste, confusion, legal liability, and ministry ineffectiveness. Organization is never to be the main thing, to be sure, but it's an essential thing blessed by God when it works well on behalf of the main thing, the church's evangelistic mission. God covenants with called and obedient children. In such a partnership, God can and does work through church organization as well as outside it.

A consultant once described the Movement paradoxically. It desires an effective unity among all God's people but perceives that any centralized authority is unacceptable. The resulting dilemma is the "intellectual desire for the benefits of centralization, which runs parallel and contrary to an emotional resistance to centralization."[119] The problem now faced is not the Movement's large number of ministerial entities, but the functional (missional) weakness they have because of the absence of cohesion and efficiency. This historic dilemma persists and often is painful for the Movement.

Project Imagine

The Movement, through its "Project Imagine" study in 2017-2018, sought some middle ground in this organizational dilemma. Its task necessarily proceeded in the prevailing context of the two central and contrasting values treasured by the Movement. They form a pivotal and persisting paradox in the Movement's very DNA. They are the ongoing attempt to balance *freedom* and *accountability*, taking human hands off the controls of God's church while also seeking to unite all believers for the fulfillment of the church's mission.

As Project Imagine began seeking a more desirable pattern of increased accountability in the Movement's mission together in the United States and Canada, the expected happened. There was the paradox, unity, yes, but not at the expense to our precious freedom. The resulting challenge is like this old saying. "When you come to a fork in the road, take it!" Autonomy-accountability is a difficult dual fork in the Movement's past and present road.

The eventual result of the 2017-2018 "Roundtable" process of Project Imagine focused on two modest strategic initiatives, each designed to move the church beyond "today's fractured approach to Kingdom advance that cannot be materially or spiritually sustained." It's hoped that they are only the beginning of meaningful positive steps forward.

The Movement was born on the edge of the American frontier. It inherited a sense of freedom both from its sociological and biblical roots. Sometimes this sense of freedom has been allowed to overwhelm the sense of unity in Christ, a truth even more central to the meaning of the Movement. At times freedom in Christ, just as Paul warned (Gal. 5:13), has degenerated into a false and hurtful independence. Today must be a time when this blind alley no longer is allowed to prevail, restricting progress on the church's main thing, the call to spread the good news in Christ to the whole world.

It's God's church, of course, but it's also the responsibility of its members to be good stewards of the church's life and mission. We are to be God's church *together*, not a loosely connected group of autonomous believers doing as they individually please and cooperating only when their individual purposes are served. Flying off in all uncoordinated ministry directions may be a fine theoretical gesture to the freedom of the Spirit, but it's also an irresponsible way of encouraging the church to crash and burn!

Disciples aren't to organize *the church*, but they are to organize and handle well *its ministries*. Daniel Warner was right back in 1878. Church organizations can be an obstacle to God's work. He was not quite right, however, by then assuming that avoiding all church organizing would definitely be an enhancement of God's work. It's not!

NEEDED CONVERSATION AND ACTION

1. The Church of God Movement is anything but a "Pope" people, although it was somewhat that way in the first two or three generations of its life. Have you known an unusually influential leader in the church's life? In the absence of formal authority structures, isn't it inevitable that the strongest personality will have the greatest influence?

2. Who's really in charge in the Movement, if anyone? "Independency" is so valued that someone chosen to lead appears mistrusted and re-

sisted if he/she actually tries to lead. Isn't a high valuing of "autonomy" at odds with the very meaning of being the church together?

3. What of the common observation that the forward progress of the Movement has been blocked by constant fear? The Movement often has resisted involvement with Christians who haven't seen the "light" on the church. Has that been because of fear that such involvement might erode the Movement's witness—guilt by association? Is fear of being "like the denominations" an obstacle to the progress of the Movement today?

4. A definite organizational change was the General Assembly's recent decision to take full control of the Movement's ministerial credentialing in the United States and Canada. It authorized an official *Credentials Manual*, established a standing "Committee on Credentials," and empowered this COC to implement, interpret, and revise the Manual as it judged wise in the future. Many were nervous about such "power" threatening the supposed full autonomy of the Movement's regional assemblies. Were these necessary steps on behalf of fairness and legal protection or an "overreach from Anderson"?

5. What role should national church leaders play in guiding the mission emphases of the Movement's assemblies and congregations? What role should Church of God Ministries play in stimulating, resourcing, and guiding the ministries of the Movement in North America, and even around the world?

6. Should organizing activities in church life be going on at all? Does the Spirit of God work best outside organized church bodies, or might the Spirit work just as well, maybe even better, in settings where believers are active stewards of the callings, giftings, and resources they have received?

7. Why was the recent "Roundtable" process of Project Imagine as difficult as it was? What is there about the Movement's core commitments that impedes progress in organizing effectively its corporate life? Should this be changed? If so, how can it be done?

The
Church
that God
Intends

Reconsidering the Reformation Heritage
of the Church of God (Anderson)

Barry L. Callen

Chapter

CHURCH REFORM
AND MISSION

The main thing for the church is worshipping God and then hallowing his holy name by receiving, exhibiting, and sharing the good news in Jesus Christ—conversion, discipleship, evangelism, and sacrificial service to all of humankind. In the next chapter we will focus on the servant dimensions of being agents of activating God's kingdom here and now. But first, we must be careful to balance properly the call to church reform and the many other tasks of church life.

The first work of the church is vertical, confronting God in humility, repentance, and then grateful worship. In other words, the church first must *become the church*. That's essential for the church's effective witness to the world. Jesus said that people will know you are my disciples only when you have a love for each other that could only be a gift of God (Jn. 13:35). When that love is received and embodied, the church then can turn horizontally to bring the loving life of God's kingdom to bear on the surrounding society. Reaching outward without first having reached upward usually means that church and social reform efforts will resemble the current culture of the world as much as the kingdom of God.

Pioneers of the Church of God Movement recognized this sequence of the vertical prior to the horizontal. They saw the Christian church community around them seriously compromised, organizing and acting unlovingly more like the world than the kingdom of God. This compromise had to be addressed first. They sought to better align the church to God's expectations of holiness and unity. The church first must *be the church*, a loving, holy, and united community of the redeemed, before it can be an adequate instrument of God for reaching others.

It is admitted that the views, attitudes, and actions of the Movement's pioneers were not always above question, but at least their instinct was in the right direction. Right relationships with God and then loving unity with each other as believers are critical for then seeking to accomplish the mission of the church in any time and place.

Form Follows Function

When a congregation plans a new program or facility or set of bylaws, it's generally agreed that form should follow function. That is, the purpose envisioned should dictate the design of how it is to be implemented. In the history of the Church of God Movement, there has been considerable focus on the issue of faulty church forms ("denominationalism") and their needed change. Has this focus on *form* supplanted the *function* priority?

At the Movement's beginning the focus on form involved a vigorous critiquing of the organizational waywardness of the established Christian bodies of that time. The "sects" were denounced for allowing human forms to dominate and even strangle the church's very life and intended mission. Then, after a few generations of the Movement's life, there came the unexpected struggle of having to deal with some emerging forms within its own life. This emergence, of course, was resisted, and to a considerable degree still is. This emergence and resistance raise a key and complex question.

What exactly is the main thing around which all else in the church should revolve? The earliest life of the Movement tended to suggest the central need for *church reform*. How could the core mission of the church be accomplished when hampered by the heavy control of human hands? The first need was seen to be calling on all Christians to "come out" of the sectish mire of denominationalism. Then, and only then, could come renewed emphasis on the main thing, conversion, discipleship, and evangelism. Only when the church finally is released from her paralyzing compromises will she be free to be her true self and about her true mission.

This call for freedom from wayward church establishments led the Church of God Movement to being called a "reformation movement." The word "reformation" was understood less as re-forming what was and more as demolishing the church establishments altogether and beginning from scratch. This, of course, soon brought the dilemma of an active "dis-establishment" mentality being dominant in the Movement's early life. This, of course, would slowly change as the Movement became more established itself. New generations of its people would share less the original call to "come out" from the human mess that the pioneers had seen sickening church life.

Beginning with Fear and Distrust

Daniel S. Warner had been separated from his original home denomination in a way that soured him on organized churches in general. Later he acted to separate himself even from the mainstream of the Holiness Movement over an organizational disagreement. He resisted denominational membership being required for participation in holiness renewal efforts. His focus was on Christian holiness, but his passion was on linking the purifying potential of holiness to a recovered Christian unity of the church in advance of Christ's soon return. People needed sanctified, yes, but *so did the church*!

This reforming passion of Warner was rooted in negative church experiences he had encountered personally. The detail of his troubled journey is found in his biography, *It's God's Church!* This journey helped paint the resulting Movement as a church-reforming crusade. The Movement's fixation on the evils of institutionalized Christianity would be its glory and its agony. The reform in view was nothing short of a dismantling of denominationalism.

Christians were called out of the "sects" and urged to forsake "Babylon" (the apostate denominational world). Envisioned was a "cleansing of the sanctuary," the "last reformation" of the church. Warner's drive came to be church reform. This preoccupation inevitably interfered to some degree with the church's main thing, conversion, discipleship, and evangelism.

Today this picture has changed considerably. Note that typically this church body now is referred to as the "Church of God Movement," with the word "reformation" often dropped. That's because in more recent generations there has been little emphasis on the Movement consciously attempting to impact the structural life of the broader church beyond an occasional critique of it. "Thrashing Babylon" is now a reforming preoccupation largely relegated to the Movement's past.

The fear of church "organization" and the hesitancy to invest real "authority" in church leaders clearly remain, but now there is little harsh rhetoric aimed at the threatening evils of surrounding "denominationalism." The world of the denominations has weakened and the high ground of the Movement hardly being one itself isn't that clear anymore. The dramatic reform of today's established churches is the preoccupation of very few in today's Movement. More time and energy is being invested by the Movement in its own internal issues, and even its survival in these very new and demanding times.

There has been a general backing away from the stridency of Warner's anti-organizational attitudes. The focus shift has been described by historian Charles E. Brown as moving from the "leader principle" (strong individuals gifted by God, with little organization necessary) to "spiritual democracy" (decision-making and cooperation by the larger body). By the 1930s Brown was seeing as a serious error the pioneers relying on "charismatic" governance—leadership by a few gifted individuals of particular prominence. Abandoning control by individuals "freed the next generation of Movement leadership from a slavish adherence to the past."[120]

Russell R. Byrum once commented, "Uncle Enoch owned the church. There was only one roster of the saints, the *Gospel Trumpet* subscription list, and he alone had access to it."[121] That owning was more than a century ago, an earlier time when the Movement was small and its "programming" minimal. Today the picture is very different. The Movement is established in dozens of countries and its ministry bodies are numerous, although their networking remains minimal at best.

Organizational fear and distrust of leaders unfortunately continue. Commitment to "autonomy" remains strong. Therein lies the Movement's glory and agony. Church reform remains on the broad agenda, at least in theory, but these days it hardly impacts the awareness of most congregational members. Their concerns are more likely to be local. If there is any crusading going on, it's probably more about preferences of music styles in worship than on some past vision of church-wide division and desperately needed reform.

What about the "Main Thing"?

One truth is clear. For the spiritual health and mission effectiveness of the church, the organizational question is an important one, but it's not *the main thing.* Jesus said virtually nothing about church organization and made clear that he had not come to disrupt or abandon his own Jewish heritage. Granted, he was critical of some of the "traditions of the elders," but his passion was on the arriving reign of his Father coming wonderfully near in his own life and ministry. This was the good news and it was to transform lives and be shared widely.

The emerging church seen in the New Testament was not "in search of a perfect organization as an end in itself. Instead, it was devoted to the spread of the gospel, to maturing in the life of Christ, and to the development of a unified witness to the world."[122] There's the main thing! In Christ there is good news and the church is to receive, embody, and spread this news. Discipleship is about becoming living models of the good news of God for us in Christ. Evangelism is about sharing this good news as widely and effectively as possible.

For the earliest Christians, here's what Jesus said should come first. We are to wait on the arrival of the presence and power of the Spirit of God. Only by that coming are we enabled to become "Pentecost people," people formed, governed, and sent on mission by the Spirit. Being such people will result in our focusing on the Great Commission of sharing the good news with all the world. God was with us and for us in Jesus! Patterns, procedures, and programs of church life are significant, but only as they serve well this good-news spreading.

The main thing for the church is the *becoming* of believers (conversion and holiness) and then the *going* of believers, getting out the good-news message (discipleship and evangelism). This message is the core biblical story and mandate. God created, now has been with us in Jesus, remains with us in the Spirit of Jesus, seeks the reconciling of all that hell has spoiled, and one day will conclude this time-space world in judgment and justice. Meanwhile, God's people are to live in hope, grow in grace, and share the good news for the potential salvation of all people.

The earliest leaders of the Movement would never have argued with this main thing, not at all! Still, it appears that they were often focused elsewhere. They certainly were sincere Christian people thrilled with the grace of God and caring deeply about the well-being of lost souls. Even so, they saw little time available for discipleship development or the huge task of world mission. Christ was coming soon and the task immediately at hand was purifying the corrupted church in readiness for Christ's arrival to claim his Bride. Believers were to be freed from the church's apostasy. The focus was on church *reformation* as much or even more than on evangelistic *proclamation*.

Pioneers of the Movement cried out for change, for removing human hands from the throat of God's church. As the biography of the Movement's primary pioneer captures in its title, *It's God's Church!*[123] These visionary voices critiqued especially all episcopal forms of church organization (power most centralized in a few) and opted for the congregational style of structure (power most localized with as little empowered leadership "outside" as possible). How, they constantly asked, can anyone become a mature disciple or proclaim with integrity and freedom the pure gospel of Christ while enslaved in a humanly-controlled denomination?

Therefore, church reform was a highlighted goal of the Movement from its beginning. The launching insight of Daniel Warner's 1878 journal entry was: "The Lord showed me that holiness could never prosper upon sectarian soil encumbered by human creeds and party names." Holiness was critical, but apparently radical church reform was the problem to be faced first.

To be clear again, for the early leaders of the Movement, the main thing, spreading the good news of the saving gospel of Christ, was never in question. This is clear from the 1920 booklet *Look on the Fields* by F. G. Smith. It's a report of the Missionary Board of the Movement and progress of mission outreach in Japan, China, Fiji Islands, Australia, India, Egypt, Syria, Europe, British West Indies, Canal Zone, and South America. Being profusely illustrated with photos of reaching love and compassion for human misery, there is no question about the Movement's evangelistic zeal.

Even so, human denominationalism was seen as obstructing effective evangelism. That intolerable obstruction was being addressed dramatically by God through this Movement just prior to the return of the Son. The urgent task was the necessary reform of the wayward "churches." Warner had begun preaching Christian holiness, hoping to bring new life to individuals and the churches. When that was not well received, he chose to "come out," seeking the needed church reformation beyond the badly infected "sectarian soil." The "last reformation" was on![124]

Freed from Hurtful *Isms*

The pioneers of the Church of God Movement were surely right about one thing. The church is a divine organism, a living body of believers, a holy "movement," the body of God's redeemed people. This body must not be forced into institutionalized forms or any other human preoccupation that distracts from the church's primary nature and mission. That mission is evangelism, discipleship development, and world mission.

The Movement's pioneers were wrong, however, at one key point at least. They were wrong about the immediacy of their end-time expectation and in their interpretation of biblical "prophecy." These inappropriate assumptions helped take them heavily into a preoccupation with urgent church reform. These end-time and church-reform preoccupations tended to undercut a primary focus on discipleship development and evangelism. After all, there was no time for these, and Christian education was being used by denominations mostly as a tool for their own preservation as self-serving organizations. That had to end, and as quickly as possible.

By the 1940s it had become clearer that what early Movement pioneers had reacted against, excessive institutionalizing of the church, may not be the exact problem of the church. It's the *"ism"* aspect of denominational*ism* and creedal*ism* that diverts believers down wrong paths. Being in Christ should spell death to human "isms" in general—national*ism*, rac*ism*, gender*ism*, class*ism*, etc. We are all to be one in Christ. Being freed from hurtful *isms* is to be released to be excited and unified representatives of the coming kingdom of God.

Now into the twenty-first century, especially in the modern West, *independency* has come to dominate the general culture. It's increasingly obvious to some Movement leaders that an extreme congregational*ism* is yet another "ism" in conflict with the church's main thing. The church as a united body suffers when its many parts begin going their separate ways and leadership beyond the local level is distrusted and sometimes refused altogether. Insisting that the only allowable church organization is direct rule of the Spirit can be as chaotic and ineffective as it is admirable and appropriate in principle.

In 2019 my wife and I attended the fifteenth annual meeting of the Wesleyan Holiness Connection hosted by the Salvation Army in its international headquarters in London, England. We toured the founding ministry sites of William and Catherine Booth and John Wesley, supplemented by commentary from top leaders of both the Army and Methodism. I was reminded forcefully of how much the Church of God Movement is in debt to these two major Christian holiness and reformation bodies.

The Army likely would never have existed if the Church of England had been ministering effectively among the very poor in East London and in various industrial and mining locations across England. The main thing, compassion and evangelism, must be extended to all, and the poor will never hear well the message of evangelists who are not prepared to care for their most basic human needs. The Army has demonstrated clearly that a highly organized body of Christians can serve well the message and sacrificial mission of Christ.

Methodism was not intended to be a new denominational reality. John Wesley was a loyal Anglican priest who nonetheless was disturbed by certain of that church's significant failures. He sought to reform from within the church body he loved. A complex set of dynamics intervened and led to a separation, an unintended "coming out" of the Church of England and the formation of the separate Methodist body. Warner associated briefly with the later Holiness Movement that intended to revive a stagnated Methodism, but he rebelled at its maintenance of the denominational system that he judged part of the problem. Time has shown his judgment questionable.

The way now ahead for the Movement involves a careful determination of priorities, sometimes different from the past. For instance, church organization (1) must not be denied as legitimate (God works through as well as outside organizations), (2) must function so as to not violate the primacy of the Holy Spirit in the church's life, (3) must be capable of gathering the personnel and resources available and arranging them for their most efficient use, and (4) must engage these gathered resources in the service of the main things, evangelism, discipleship development, and world mission.

As Methodism has rightly insisted, the overarching goal is spreading "Scriptural holiness" across the land. As the Salvation Army has well shown, such spreading can be served well by careful church organization. The Spirit of Jesus is the Heart and Guide and Power of the church. The person and accomplished work of Jesus is the central Subject. The structures and strategies of the church's life and ministries are necessary, and they must be adjusted as times change and the wind of the Spirit blows. Faith must overcome fear, allowing the church to both believe and build.

The Movement that God intends to inspire today is one that is properly cautioned about over-structuring church life, but one that no longer is so organizationally gun-shy that it chooses to let the mission languish if necessary. Spreading Scriptural holiness across the land is absolutely essential. It's very Wesleyan and, more importantly, very biblical. The Bible teaches a holy experience that reflects God's character to the world. This experience enables a unity between individual believers and even among church bodies, a unity that makes the church's mission increasingly possible.

Ongoing church reform is often necessary to better enable God's mission to proceed. Today the Church of God Movement is facing some needed internal reform of its own. Adjusting patterns of church life is part of it. More basic is being infused with the motivating power of Scriptural holiness that motivates and guides all change in God's desired direction. That direction is not searching the skies for signs of the end times but searching the streets of this troubled world for the needs that the arriving kingdom of God is prepared to meet through a faithful church. Tomorrow's reign of God is to be activated today by the church.

NEEDED CONVERSATION AND ACTION

1. If the main thing for the church is the Christ-like *becoming* of believers (conversion and holiness) and then the Spirit-inspired *going* of believers, getting out the good-news message (discipleship and evangelism), how do you think you and your church are doing in these areas? How could the priorities of your congregation be strengthened?

2. What is the difference between "independence" and "interdependence" in church life? Which do you see being emphasized in the Bible? Are autonomy and unity both biblical and compatible?

3. The Bible teaches a "community" of believers, members in covenant

with God and each other. How can a local congregation model and fulfill the command of Christ for unity and interdependence among disciples on common mission?

4. Pioneers of the Movement cried out for change, for removing human hands from the throat of God's church. Given the circumstances they faced, were they right? Given the church's present circumstances, is such a cry for removing human hands still justified as a priority?

5. Distrust of government and leadership is rampant in today's Western culture. Has such distrust inappropriately found its way into the church? Are the church's vision and mission being hurt by such distrust? What can be done to diminish the negative impact of anything that fights against a united church intentionally together on mission to the whole world?

6. The Church of God began as a "reform movement." So much has changed since that beginning. Are reform movements themselves ever in need of biblical reform and realignment? How do you think that today's Church of God Movement could benefit from this discussion of the "main thing"?

7. Recall the earlier reform ministries of the Salvation Army and Methodism in England, including their strong commitment to spiritual discipline and organization as essentials of church life. The Church of God Movement historically is in debt to these prominent Christian revival and reform movements. What might they have to teach the Movement today?

Chapter 12

GOD'S KINGDOM HERE AND NOW!

The Church of God Movement has always believed that becoming "born again" is an essential step to the "abundant life." But it also has contended that Jesus calls disciples to more, to holiness, a life of Christ-like compassion empowered by the Holy Spirit. The title of Max Gaulke's 1959 book has it right. *Thy Kingdom Come—Now!* To be a faithful follower of Jesus requires becoming "supernatural instruments in the redemptive, daring, radical, world-changing, life-altering, risk-assuming way of Jesus in this world."[125] The future belongs to God, and so does the present!

Too many Christians think of their faith only in terms of private spiritual healing and inspiration. But in God's plan there's a larger social and even political agenda. A person's faith that remains private "will never end up as the Bible ends with 'a new heaven and a new earth' and the New Jerusalem descending to live among humans (Rev. 21:1-3)."[126] John Wesley said it numerous times and Church of God leaders have always known it. Believers are called to *inward* transformation and a resulting *outward* practice of mercy and justice.

Recall the list in chapter seven of the Movement's theological perspectives judged worthy of sharing with today's global church. Let me repeat two of them in brief.

1. Expectations of end-time events should be tempered by humility and disciplined by the clear biblical mandate to focus on *the present mission of the church.*

2. The resurrection of Jesus was the beginning of God's ongoing project of infusing *this fallen world* with the life of heaven.

The mission of the church is to be more than getting people to heaven. It's also to fill this fallen world with a foretaste of heaven. The goal of *then* includes making a difference *now.* God's kingdom has come near in Jesus and that nearness is to be activated through the life and ministries of the church. Since some early Movement leaders sought perspective in the Book of Revelation, note this good perspective drawn partly from that biblical source:

> In the day of the Lord, God reclaims the universe. The Bible calls us to transformation, not speculation. It calls us to make a hard turn in discipleship with new lifestyle choices rather than compromised collaboration or apathy with a system about to fail. We pull ourselves free from the systems and structures that have caused us to lose sight of God's kingdom. We walk with God in white. "Whoever has ears, let them hear" (Matt. 11:15 and 13:9, Rev. 13:9).[127]

Discipleship focus is to be on the *now.* The biblical call is to *present transformation* of ourselves and our world. It's not to future speculation and pushing the pause button until God finally makes all things right as we gladly look on. Christians must resist the temptation to reach for the raw excitement of claiming to know what's coming next, exactly when Jesus will return, and how all things will work out in the end. In fact, we really don't know much about these future things, and Jesus clearly drew our attention away from the ultimate future and to the present and its urgent mission.

The early Church of God Movement experienced real excitement when key biblical interpreters explained the symbols of the Book of Revelation, spotted the Movement itself, and thrilled at being heralds of the final day. That was more speculation than divine revelation. Now that earlier thrill must be replaced with the thrill of Jesus announcing that in his presence the kingdom has come near and there *now* is a world to save by the spreading of the good news!

That good news goes beyond personal salvation. God the Judge will determine all things in the end. In the meantime, children of the Divine are to be both recipients of and then active agents of transformation. We are to work for reconciliation and justice in our time and social settings, doing so in the name of our Lord and through the power of his Spirit now graciously alive in us. The Movement's pioneers were especially concerned about the dangers of denominationalism. More dangerous in today's church setting appears to be nationalism and consumerism and individualism. The church is to be a prophetic voice to the culture, not a subtle reflection of its current wayward preoccupations.

Instruments of God

Church reform? Yes, without question there is such an urgent need from time to time. This has been and should continue to be part of what the Church of God Movement is all about. The church, the body of Christ today, needs to regain its integrity in the public eye (holiness) and its wholeness (unity). It also must be on guard against any disabling self-preoccupation (denominational*ism*).

Then what about evangelism, discipleship development, and world mission? Yes, absolutely! These are what God always wants the church to be doing. The church should be nurturing new disciples into spiritual maturity and productiveness and spreading the redeeming good news of God in Jesus Christ for the whole world. When properly reformed and in good health, holy and united, the church is at her best for accomplishing God's will in the present time.

Is there still more expected of the church? Yes, there's still more. The people of Christian faith are at their best only when they are holy and united and when they are envisioning, strategizing, and working toward the realization of a reconciled church and world. The Christian community is called to be an agent of Jesus, an instrument of God, doing as Jesus did through the power of his Spirit. For both individuals and social systems, the church is to be seeking to bring to bear *now* the reconciling and redeeming presence of the kingdom of God. The whole of human society stands in need of the renewing grace of God.

Some of the early leaders of the Movement strayed too far into future speculation by using the Book of Revelation to explain the whole of church history and justify the Movement's own existence. That straying, however, gave way over time to a more Jesus-like instinct. Focus for the serious Christian believer is to be away from future speculation and any self-serving reading of the biblical text. Instead, focus is to be on the difficult demands of present ministry in a fallen world that's so loved by God.

As the current General Director of Church of God Ministries says, we are to become nothing less than "supernatural instruments in the redemptive, daring, radical, world-changing, life-altering, risk-assuming way of Jesus." As an historian of the Movement once put it, "Our noncreedal position commits us to a practical approach to Christian doctrine, i.e., practice trumps belief statements."[128] We are to be, believe, *and do*.

Practice, indeed. We are to be enacting on the streets and back alleys and courtrooms of today's world the reconciling and renewing grace of God. The fullness of truth comes to be known well by the believer only when that truth is put into self-sacrificial practice. Witness to Jesus becomes credible to others only when the messenger displays a loving Christ-likeness that seeks justice for all.

Activating God's Kingdom

Leaders of the Church of God Movement over the generations have been quite consistent in their view of one important matter, the future and its proper relationship to the present. Believers are commissioned to be redemptive forerunners of God's future that already is breaking into the present. For the Christian community, it arrived dramatically in the life, death, and resurrection of Jesus. Now it's *to keep coming* through the ministry of the Spirit of Jesus active in the faithfulness of God's people.

To be with God tomorrow (heaven) is clearly related to being about God's business today (mission). Salvation is not based on works. Nonetheless, it's hardly real without them. To be alive in Christ is to begin acting like Christ. "Serious discipleship takes priority over speculative dispensationalism; the significance of Pentecost far outweighs ponderings about purgatory, premillennialism, and the perseverance of the saints. The call from the God of the future, and the foundation for participating in God's future, necessarily involves participating in the present work of the Spirit in fashioning new creations."[129]

Baptism is a classic symbol of the beginning of the Christian life. In the New Testament, baptism is associated closely with receiving the saving and renewing Spirit of God. It's a sign of becoming a member of God's church and a launching into new life in the Spirit. It's the public declaration that one has determined to be enrolled in the family of God and anxious to be empowered by God's Spirit so that it becomes possible to be about the business of God in this world.

Baptismal candidates should do more than witness to an inner spiritual experience of "salvation." They also should commit to life in the body of Christ, kingdom-of-God life, "eternal" life. Such divine intervention makes a difference here and now by the power of God's Spirit in all dimensions of personal and social life. "Eternal" life means more than life that is everlasting. It also means reflecting the very life of God during our brief existence and ministry in this present world.

As the most representative body of the Movement in the United States and Canada, the General Assembly often has spoken to the church on a wide range of issues, personal and public. The intent has been to give guidance for activating the life of God in the present realities of today's troubled world. A resolution adopted by the 2019 General Assembly offers the general rationale for such speaking and calls to action. "The church is called to give witness in all arenas, with its ministry of reconciliation addressing all forms of social and spiritual oppression. We have faith in the power of Christ that calls us to **ACT**—**A**waken, **C**onfront, and **T**ransform society by embracing strategies that bring hope through social action."

The Movement, theologically conservative by most measures, has been socially "progressive" from its beginning. Characteristic of its years has been a call to freedom from domineering church institutions and all oppressors of life. There has been an exhilarating sense of spontaneous joy in the Lord and the conviction that all believers are equally a part of the one church by the gracious action of God. Classic lines of public discrimination have been denounced. These "liberating" keynotes attracted to the Movement socially oppressed people, particularly women and African-Americans to whom were granted equal access to all levels of church life and leadership.

This liberation brought persecution to the Movement's pioneers since they were upsetting prevailing social standards that contrasted with God's intentions. Jesus did and experienced the same. The church is not to wait until after the return of Christ to seek a realization of God's kingdom in this world. The *then and there* is to be our goal in the *here and now*. Whatever the obstacles or partial successes of our ministry efforts, the commission of Jesus is to make God's kingdom active and evident *now*.

Believers are freed in Christ. Our bodies and their actions are then to be understood as temples of the Holy Spirit activating God's present kingdom. Minds and hearts are to be filled and fired by God's Spirit. Christians are to avoid personal practices that are addictive and lead back to slavery. The society in general is to be encouraged to create laws that mirror God's loving will for human welfare. Accordingly, the Movement's General Assembly has spoken often over the decades on various church policies and social issues.[130]

For instance, the 1964 Assembly authorized the establishment of a Commission on Social Concerns. Why? Because "there is manifest urgency for the careful and prayerful study of ways in which articulate calls may be given to the congregations for them to carefully consider Christian responsibility in the fields of temperance and general welfare, particularly with alcohol problems, gambling, tobacco, and pornographic literature; in areas of peace and world order, particularly with military policy and legislation for conscription, disarmament, and nuclear weapon control; and in the area of human relations, particularly in race relations, civil liberties, church-state relationships, housing, and civic responsibility."

In 1979 the Movement's seminary in Anderson, Indiana, authored the *WE BELIEVE* booklet. While not "official," it was circulated and appreciated widely in that time of the Movement's centennial celebration. The booklet concludes with this fitting summary of the proper identity of the Movement:

> In devotion to Christ as the head of the church, we desire to be a biblical people, a people who worship the triune God, a people transformed by the grace of God, a people of the kingdom of God, a people committed to building up the one, universal church of God, and a people who, in God's love, *care for the whole world*.

Kingdom life, life in and through the Spirit, is a caring and loving life engaging with and seeking to redeem the whole world. Christian "eschatology" (doctrine of final things) must be more than hoping for what is yet to come. It's also a call to be *faithful in the meantime* in light of what is to come.[131]

The church should be "nothing short of the fellowship of *tomorrow's* people sharing with Christ the urgent task of re-arranging the realities of *today's* world."[132] Christian life is to be acting courageously in the present from the perspective and with the resources of the future. The church is to be a people increasingly defined by the coming kingdom of God and constantly at work on its behalf.

What the church should be, however, is hardly what it often is. From its beginning, the Movement found the established church bodies obstructing and neglecting the full mission of Christ. Too often the "churches" had become controlled by leaders encasing them in a virtual churchly museum (denominational*ism*). That's an ever-present danger of church life, including the life of the Movement itself.

The 1981 "Dialogue on Internal Unity" of the Movement announced this. "The Church of God Movement has a biblical mandate to be involved in world issues by caring and doing and cultivating greater awareness." Then the 1984 "Consultation on Mission and Ministry" of the Movement affirmed a similar goal: "To challenge the Church of God Movement to redemptive action in relation to the social issues of our time."

With this impetus and rationale, various calls for action have come from the floor of the General Assembly. All are recorded in the 2019 publication *Leaning Forward!*. There is a positive and negative attached to all such calls. The positive is that these formal resolutions are biblically inspired encouragements to needed Christian action. The negative is that any follow-up has been entirely voluntary in nature, sometimes resulting in little if anything actually happening. The Movement's visionary ministry idealism, mixed with its uncoordinated volunteerism, is part of its ongoing glory and agony.

Let's Get "Radical"!

Daniel S. Warner, primary pioneer of the Church of God Movement, was a nineteenth-century "radical" reformer in the Wesleyan/Holiness tradition. He was not inventing new truths but reaching back to the biblical foundations of the faith. He also was reaching forward for fresh applications that would bring those foundations alive in his time and place. He was following John Wesley who earlier had paired four paradoxes, each essential for authentic (biblical) and relevant (contemporary) Christian faith. These paradoxes are:

1. Sound Doctrine *and* Spiritual Experience.
2. Necessary Faith *and* Resulting Works.
3. The Individual Believer *and* the Social Environment.
4. Our Time *and* the Perspectives of God's Eternity.

These twin realities, if fully embraced, will ignite a "radical" style of Christianity. Such Christianity will dare to go to the root of things and thus be freed from the status quo of compromised church life. To be a "radical" Christian is to have: (1) an all-truth vision that is convictional without being creedal (deep belief without shallow arrogance); (2) belief with the mind while also experiencing it with the heart; (3) personal transformation in the private closet of prayer and also going on to serve in the back alleys of human need; and (4) willingness to experiment with fresh forms of church life without being slave to any (it's God's church, not ours).

God's people are to reach for *the whole,* even though they know that the fullness of truth and the completeness of its implementation exceed their reach. This keeps believers humble and always reaching. We Christians are to resist rigid church establishments and put aside the divisions caused by resulting denominational pride. We are to be open to all of our brothers and sisters in the faith and to all that the Bible has to say as the Spirit continues to reveal its depths to our waiting hearts and hands.

We who walk with Jesus are to be anchored in the truths of God's revealed yesterday and yet never imprisoned by the language or institutional forms of yesterday's church life. We are to cherish the old *and* welcome the new. After all, God remains *on the move.* We who belong to Jesus must keep moving with this mobile, on-mission God. Like in the differing days of John Wesley and Daniel Warner, in our day it's time to get "radical" again!

Living the Lord's Prayer

How easy it is for the people of God to go wrong. If not deliberately disobeying, at least followers of Jesus get off track and tend to neglect or even forget. The people of Jesus are to be active agents of God's arriving future and not more examples of the fallenness of this world, even if they are dressed in the finest religious clothes. Jesus found an alarming religious deterioration among his own people. He confronted it and they proceeded to reject him.

May we not be equally guilty today! Jesus anticipated the danger of such ongoing deterioration among his future disciples and taught us how to avoid it. Nothing, he explained, could be more important than learning how to pray for the really important things. Only that way will we learn how to live as Jesus desires. The "Lord's Prayer" is the central guide that Jesus gave us.

A key element of this pivotal Christian prayer is the subject of bread. According to Jesus, first we must honor the name of God and seek to have God's kingdom come and will be done here and now. Then we are to ask for our daily bread. For most of us in the West today, grocery stores are full and reasonably priced. Rather than crying out for needed bread, typically we make ourselves sick from eating too much. For many others in the world, however, survival depends on finding food and decent drink each day.

Jesus is telling us, his properly prayerful disciples, that bread and ministry must not be separated. The good creation of God provides everything needed for sustaining life, that is, unless it's wasted or hoarded. Christ's disciples are daily sustained by God *for the well-being of others*. Christians are to be stewards more than consumers. Jesus compared himself to bread (Jn. 6:35, 48). He is God's ultimate provision for both life now and in eternity. Regarding the provision of physical bread, as Jesus did for the hungry crowd on a hillside of Galilee, Christians are to pray that they will be sustained so that they can become bread *distributors*.

The most important words in the bread petition of the Lord's Prayer may be *us* and *our*. We are to ask God for daily bread that God intends to be *ours*. It's not *my* bread, but a corporate Divine gift. All bread is a gift from God's hand given both for nourishment and for sharing. How a believer handles bread is a sign of true discipleship and Christian holiness. "Justice, including efficient food production and equitable distribution, is a critical part of the Christian gospel and calling."[133] It's an essential aspect of living *here and now* the life of God's coming kingdom.

NEEDED CONVERSATION AND ACTION

1. Being "born again" is an essential step to "abundant life." But Jesus calls disciples to more, to a Kingdom life empowered by the Holy Spirit and directed to real changes in the world of today. Are you ready to move to the next step?

2. It's so tempting to just leave things to God and get caught up in expectations of end-time events when God will make all things right. But Jesus directs another way, to a focus on the present mission of the church. Believers must resist future speculations that distract from current ministry tasks and reconciliation possibilities. Are you resisting the temptation to default on present mission?

3. What changes or new initiatives would you support so that your congregation and the Church of God Movement as a whole could actually live out the coming of God's kingdom now, right here on earth with all of its great needs?

4. Here is a key statement in this chapter. Think seriously about what it should mean for you and your congregation. "The church, the body of Christ today, needs to regain its integrity in the public eye (holiness) and its wholeness (unity). It also must be on guard against any disabling self-preoccupation (denominationalism) if it's to be all that God intends."

5. Here's another key statement. "To be with God tomorrow (heaven) is clearly related to being about God's business today (mission). Salvation is not based on works. Nonetheless, it's hardly real without them. To be alive in Christ is to begin acting like Christ." Are you really alive in Christ? Is that obvious in how you are reacting to evil circumstances around you?

6. Kingdom life, life in and through God's Spirit, is a caring and loving life engaging and seeking to redeem the whole world. Identify one glaring social need in the public life around your congregation. Now, how can you engage it lovingly in the name of Jesus and in the power of his Spirit!

7. Are you ready to live the Lord's Prayer? What does that have to do with bread? Are you only a consumer or also a self-less distributor?

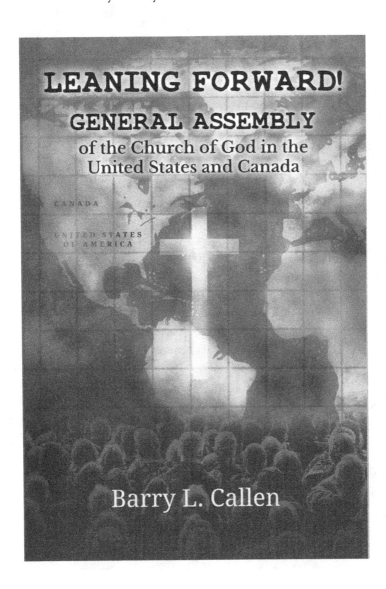

FAITHFUL IN THE MEANTIME

A BIBLICAL VIEW OF FINAL THINGS AND PRESENT RESPONSIBILITIES

Barry L. Callen

Chapter 13

KEEPING THE MOVEMENT MOVING!

So much has changed. More surely will change. If the Church of God Movement is to be true to itself, it must keep moving! Its instincts may be sound and stable, but its structures and strategies must be fluid. Otherwise, it will not remain a pliable instrument in the hands of God's Spirit for the needs of today and tomorrow. The person or church body wedded to present times soon be will a widow.

The Church of God Movement once was consciously and vigorously "anti-sectarian," in fact, "anti" almost anything characteristic of the denominational world. Some Movement leaders went so far as to judge that "the denominational world exists to justify evil under the guise of good."[134] While that was an overstatement, the relevant fact is this. The religious environment of the Movement's pioneers belongs to a distant yesterday. Now it's time to move on. Evil remains very real, but it's constantly changing faces. The Movement must not waste its energy today foolishly fighting old faces of yesterday.

Originally, the Movement trumpeted a dramatic call for reform and renewal in the Christian church world. It had no history or traditions of its own that were vulnerable to this call. That's different today. Now nearly a century and a half old itself, the Movement must also dare to look at itself when it calls for church reform and renewal. It no longer exists outside the range of needed change. It's a Movement that must keep moving or it will no longer be true to its own self.

Another fact is crucial to note. The denominational world is hardly what it once was. Therefore, it's time for the Movement to stop focusing on the limitations of others. What's especially needed now? It's a *modeling* of what God intends and will provide for a body of holy believers hungry for a united church ready for inspired world mission together. And the "together" must include the multitude of sisters and brothers in the faith who do not carry the "Church of God" label.

So much about the 1880s isn't characteristic of the church world today. The denominations are hardly what they once were, and in many ways neither is the Movement. New generations have come into the Movement, with many of today's participants knowing little or nothing about its history and particular concerns. For the sake of the future, it's time for the Church of God Movement to remember what it *was* and then seek to discover what God wishes for it to be *now*. It's time for the Movement to look back with appreciation and then move on with fresh vision!

Who Was Daniel Warner?

Today one regularly encounters the question, "Who was Daniel Warner?" It's asked by Movement people even though there is in the life of today's Movement Warner Press, Warner University, Warner Pacific University, Warner Camp, etc. Institutions featuring this name presumably carry on Daniel Warner's heritage intentionally and proudly, although most of their constituents are likely to give little if any thought to the background or continuing meaning of the name. This small fact highlights a large problem for today's Movement.

The recent booklet *The Top Ten* speaks modestly to the problem, identifying ten reasons why the primary pioneer of the Movement, Daniel S. Warner, is still relevant.[135] None of these ten reasons, however, relate to the original cry for trapped Christians to "come out" from the wayward denominations. The reasons given for relevancy all relate to aspects of Warner's own spiritual life that are exemplary for today's journeying believers.

Virtually silent in the Movement now is the old church-reformation cry to abandon the denominations and purify the Bride of Christ just before the Bridegroom's soon return. Such a cry, if made, would resonate with very few people in today's Movement pews in North America, and certainly not with many in the Movement's larger global constituency who never knew the nineteenth-century sting of American denominationalism.

Freedom from institutional control of life certainly does resonate as a motivating force in today's church and society generally. In the churches across North America, non-denominational congregations are now very common. The independents value localized control. Rarely, however, are they on a dramatic "last reformation" crusade aimed at bringing in a new structural day for the church as a whole. What, then, happens to a Movement that historically was dedicated to being a "reformation" movement when reformation is no longer high on its agenda?

Change is everywhere and a movement that isn't moving is surely stagnating. A movement by definition is dynamic, always in motion, daring to keep experimenting its way in present circumstances toward the fulfillment of God's future. Flexible freedom and contemporary relevance are hallmarks of the reforming vision of the Church of God Movement, even if not always implemented well.

The above chapters have sought to assist with theological keynotes that should characterize what it means for the Movement to be both biblically faithful and currently relevant. They are reflections of the wonderful theological and missional heritage of the Movement, although some are reshaped and freshly focused for today. They must be taken seriously if this Movement is to have a viable future in the midst of the challenges that the churches now are facing. It's time for serious conversation to begin about how and where today's Movement should be moving.

A Great Need Still Unmet

The Church of God Movement of today must intend to be more than a loose collection of essentially independent congregations held together mostly by a few fading memories and warm personal relationships. It must find a way to again be a *compelling cause*, a powerful voice to the whole church concerning its intended holiness, wholeness, and mission.

The first generations of this Movement saw themselves as privileged heralds of God's higher will for the church. Their calling was painted with the bright colors of divine destiny. Drab grey, today's dominant color, is hardly the picture of a people on an important mission for God. How can this be changed?

The most recent generations of the Movement have faced the great danger of being essentially visionless. The bright skies of yesterday have encountered cloudy days of directionless uncertainty. The result has tended to be a self-preoccupation that's mostly in a survival mode. Too much time and energy are expended addressing immediate needs, worrying about the many problems, and accommodating current and ever-changing models of "success."

Occasionally a few frustrated leaders, seeing no other light on the Movement's horizon, have tried to return to an earlier model of Movement identity, one that most judge no longer viable. Their efforts are understandable and honorable, but likely to go nowhere. The Pastors Fellowship of recent decades is sometimes thought of as an example of such reversion to the past. Sensing the vacuum of vision in the larger Movement, or even an inappropriate vision, it has sought to resurrect and rally around exciting elements of the Movement's past. Again, this is so understandable, but hardly adequate.

My own home pastor when I was young, Lillie S. McCutcheon, was a central figure in the beginning of the Pastors Fellowship in the 1970s. She wanted to elevate the dignity of the often-forgotten pastors of the smaller congregations and the continuing relevance of some of what once was, including her ongoing affirming of the earlier validation of the Movement's existence by dramatic interpretations of biblical prophecy. She was influential, compassionate, understandably loved, but hardly the future in some of her views. Even so, I benefitted greatly by her inspiring pastoral ministry. She had her finger on an urgent need that's still unmet.

The genius of the Movement's pioneers was their ability to identify and then their courage to face the particular challenges of their time and place. The urgent need facing the Movement today is much the same. It's the need for new pioneers to realize and face creatively and courageously the needs of the church in today's time and place.

The challenge before today's Movement is to do such fresh facing by being faithful to the range of biblical mandates rehearsed above. This biblical faithfulness must be rooted in but not imprisoned by the past heritage of the Movement's original pioneers. It now must be accomplished by the whole Movement, including its large global constituency that must be appreciated and networked as never before.

And further, the Movement's mission must be accomplished through an active bridging of its own life to that of the larger community of Christians. The Movement must begin to serve the larger church not by always judging its shortcomings but by championing and helping to orchestrating the much that is good.

Becoming a Bridging People

In the absence of a compelling vision, there's the natural tendency to *reach back*. What's needed now, however, is for the Church of God Movement to catch a fresh vision that centers in *reaching out* and *reaching forward*. Being serious about realizing Christian unity and mission effectiveness in our time will require high levels of maturity and commitment. The Movement finally must take the risks of really relating, actually reaching hands to the great diversity of Christian believers. This reaching must be done without fearing contamination in the process and by not arrogantly criticizing the many inadequacies of others. After all, those others now can see the Movement's own inadequacies.

Today's Movement must reach out to fellow Christians with both conviction and humility, intentionally sharing and gladly receiving. This will require doing the difficult work of bridge-building that the Movement always has espoused and yet has seldom done. It necessitates being world Christians who aren't tied to the American culture as somehow inherently superior. It requires not seeing the church in North America as the primary center and shaper of the Movement of tomorrow. It requires both honoring the Movement's pioneers of yesterday and being new pioneers for today.

My wife and I just completed a voyage on the Mississippi River from its ending at the Gulf of Mexico to its beginnings far to Minnesota's north. It's a long water world of levies, barges, boats, and locks, with many lovely scenes and often muddy waters. The nation's commerce depends in significant part on keeping this river's heavy traffic moving, not only on but above the river. There are many bridges that enable the constant flow of cars, trucks, and trains from one shore to the other. All of this presents a good picture of the church in today's world, the church as it ought to be.

God is a covenant-making God, linking divine intentions and related human responsibilities. God is a bridge-builder, a reconciler spanning our deep human divides and making newly possible the free flow of life, fellowship, and service. It's now time for the Church of God Movement to begin thinking of itself in this way. If I were to attempt a new mission statement for the Movement, it would be something like this:

> *The Church of God Movement today is being called to be a Spirit-transformed holy people, a God-sent bridging people, a medium of reconciliation within the larger body of Christ. It's to be a mediating instrument of the Spirit that constantly encourages the free flow of the Spirit's gifts and ministries among and through all of God's called people on behalf of the whole world.*

The Movement always has affirmed the slogan, "We reach our hands in fellowship to every blood-washed one." It now should be doing just that, not with judgment of others but with humility and constructive courage. The Movement must adjust to today, a time not initially thought would even be. The needed adjustment involves moving beyond the early "anti" stance to one of bridging to and building with the "churches" that have not gone away. Today's Movement must initiate actions that move from critiquing the wrong to cooperatively constructing the right.

To do such unifying reaching involves taking a bridging posture and acting like what Movement stalwarts Gilbert W. Stafford and James Earl Massey said and did so well, namely, "I belong to the whole church and the whole church belongs to me!" They reached, related, linked, found common cause, and sought to serve the world together with all Christian brothers and sisters.

These wonderful brothers are now gone, but their witness remains. Their daring bridging efforts have shown the way to Christian networking regardless of church affiliation or minor variations of doctrine and practice. Christian unity will never be uniformity of thinking and acting. No matter. Love covers all and sends all into reaching, linking, and redeeming ministries.

Accentuate the Positive

The Church of God Movement began heavily on the negative side of things, condemning a church world judged loaded with wrongs. At first it was assumed by Movement pioneers that there was little time left before the return of Christ. The immediate tasks were to get free of the accumulated apostasy and get the freed church ready for the glorious end. Much now has changed. Christ has not returned and the Movement is being forced to deal with its own history and "traditions."

The Movement now must shift more to the positive side, daring to embody the ideals it has proclaimed for generations. The Movement always has held a great positive. It's pointed to God's alternative to church failure. God wants a church standing free of all the evil sometimes carried on in lovely buildings and with elevated religious language and rituals. The prophet Amos was brutally clear about such things a long time ago.

It's time for the Movement to recognize and admit that in some ways it's become part of that imperfect church world. That to which the Movement has called others it now must reach for itself. Reaching to others in humble reconciliation can help the Movement find itself. The positive vision of God's ideal for the church has been more a theoretical vision of the Movement than a modeled reality.[136] It's been proclaimed with power but realized only partially. The vision at first called for a dramatic process of *coming out*. There now has to be considerably more commitment to *reaching out*.

As early as 1924, H. M. Riggle saw the awkward tension between the ideal and the practical, the envisioned and the unrealized. "It was not difficult for those who clearly discerned the body of Christ to hold before the people the ideal church of the New Testament *from a purely doctrinal standpoint*. But it has become clear that it is quite another thing to demonstrate in a practical way the ideal presented."[137] Riggle's keen insight was timely then and critical now.

Daniel Warner, the Movement's primary pioneer, was an evangelist, poet, dreamer, and idealist. He didn't live long enough for us to learn if he also was a practical builder who might have moved the dream well along to practical reality. That would be left to others, and now to us. Criticism of the rest of the Christian community must shift to the rigor of actually implementing the alternative to what has been done poorly by others, and now in some ways has been done inadequately by the Movement itself.

Church reformation is a never-ending business. As the burden shifts to us, we must not fail to follow Warner is certain ways. For instance, we still should add poetry to the prose of church life, spiritual power to the programs, music to all ministry strategies. We should dance with joy as well as think through our theologies. Movement people always have been and always should be visionary dreamers and excited singers ready with testimonies of experienced new life in Christ.

Doctrine should never be merely theorized, but also internalized, experienced, sung, and lived out practically on the troubled streets of our world. The church's mission can never be accomplished by the Movement itself. Today's Movement must learn to reach its hands and build working and serving relationships with a diverse range of brothers and sisters in the faith who have no previous identification with the Movement. Church labels aren't the point, Christ is! See the Appendix for a personal testimony.

Often in the 1950s I heard Johnny Mercer sing these catchy words: "Accentuate the positive, eliminate the negative, latch on to the affirmative, don't mess with mister-in-between." Now I claim these words for the Church of God Movement. It's time to move from the negative to the positive. For too long the Movement has accentuated the negative—we are not "denominational," not "Catholic," not "Evangelical," not "Fundamentalist," not part of the human compromises that have burdened the church for centuries.

Now it's time to eliminate focus on these negatives, all defensive judgments on Christian brothers and sisters. It's time to accentuate the wonderful positives of the faith. All believers belong to Jesus by God's grace; all belong to all others who belong to the Lord; we happily reach our hearts and hands to our brothers and sisters across denominational lines and across the globe; we accept the diversity in Christ's body as enrichment and not threat; we are opposed to walls dividing followers of Jesus; we are Spirit-inspired bridge builders within Christ's fellowship and from it to the needy world.

In short, the Movement must choose to mess no longer with mister-in-between. It must not exist behind walls of minor doctrines and optional practices and human preferences that so easily divide. Movement people are to be bridge-builders, believers who accentuate the positives. And what are these positives? They are still holiness and unity, wholeness of new life in Christ and togetherness in Christ's mission, first to the whole body of Christ and then, *together*, in redemptive service to the whole world!

At the Crossroads

Pilgrims often mix their gratitude with times of questioning and murmuring. Exodus 17:1-7 is the classic model of God's people wondering whether the Lord was still with them as their journey moved into a difficult and seemingly endless wilderness. Was there really a future, a continuing cause and the divine resources to accomplish it? A wonderful land was promised, yes, but was it only an ideal not likely to become real? That kind of question now confronts the Church of God Movement. Frontiers are hard to reach when one is wandering in a vast wilderness.

The enduring concerns of the Movement remain holiness and unity, integrity and reconciliation, restored relationship with God (holiness) and with other believers (unity), all for the sake of the Christian mission in this world. These concerns have proven important and enduring, although their realization remains elusive. Today's church world cries out for someone to embrace and model them well.

Two decades into the twenty-first century, the Movement is at a crossroads. It suffers from the loss of a clear self-understanding in today's setting. Being a "movement" is a concept deeply ingrained in this reform tradition, as opposed to it being just another divisive "denomination." But exactly what is a church movement?

The word is neither biblical nor theological. It's a sociological term referring to a group within a larger whole motivated to bring needed change to that whole. It's a group not self-focused but focused on improving the larger body of which it is a part. The Church of God Movement is a body of believers that shares the motivating vision of a critical need for change in the church at large. Movement people must determine to "move together" to make it happen. They must be willing to make waves and create tension to enable the needed change in the larger body's commitments and agenda. Creating waves, however, must be done humbly. Bridge traffic must be allowed to go both ways.

The needed change in today's Christian community as a whole is this. Believers must be freed from staid, self-serving, ingrown church institutions wrongly called "churches" (God has only one church). This freedom is intended to make possible a network of relationships among the whole family of believers that is alive, flexible, united, and mission-driven. Form is not the crucial matter. Most crucial are proper church functions, desired results, and God-enabled transformations.

What's the current crossroads being faced by the "Reformation" Movement of the Church of God? It's finding some way around the current impasse. The problem is that the Movement now is hardly a distinctive fellowship within God's universal church. It's no longer a goal-directed fellowship that's moving together with a united determination to bring a particular change to the church world-wide.

If not a united and focused movement within the larger church, what has the Movement become? It's now more of a loosely connected association of primarily independent congregations lacking clear awareness of any particular contribution they are convinced God has called them to make to the whole body of Christ. It has become a standard part of the Christian landscape.

The Movement is spending considerable time and energy in survival mode. There has been a series of recent institutional crises within the Movement that have drained away valuable time, energy, and resources. Fear still haunts the halls, fear of change, fear of contamination, fear of real leadership, fear of losing independent control, fear of becoming another denomination.

This Movement has been distracted by a lack of clear identity and further injured by existing in a time of a society-wide lessening of trust in established institutions, religious or otherwise. Loyalty to "mainline" churches, something the Movement always has sought to counter, has deteriorated. Such deterioration is also affecting "sideline" reform bodies like the Church of God Movement. The universities of the Movement now have a sharply lessened percentage of students enrolling from its own congregations, with relatively few of them intending after graduation to engage in Christian ministry within the Movement.

The changing picture on the educational campuses is but a reflection of the typical congregation of the Movement today, at least in North America. Increasingly, each congregation is "doing its own thing" in doctrine, practice, mission, ministries, and worship, with "independent autonomy" a treasured value—what some recent leaders have called a "cancer" in the body of the Movement.

This fragmentation is the opposite of a conscious effort to be a united reflection of a larger reformation movement with an urgent and clear purpose under God for the whole church in this time. Gilbert Stafford properly concluded that this is "a spiritual problem that ignores the strong biblical emphasis on the interconnectedness of the people of

God."[138] It undercuts the essential meaning of being a purpose-driven "movement." Where's the hope? A path must be found from problem to solution.

From Problem to Solution

Pointing out an obvious problem is easier than announcing an adequate solution. There is no magic pill to swallow. In the chapters above, we have tried to identify crucial subjects that, if carefully redefined and re-focused, can help the Church of God Movement find its proper future. Nothing will be quick and easy, but the alternative to vigorous effort in these directions (reverting backward or doing nothing) will spell the eventual end of the Movement.

The Movement still has a chance to become a representative of what God is about in our time. Difficult or not, failing to engage God's present agenda carries much too high a price. If the Movement will dare to begin moving with God, and together, it will have to do at least these things:

> ➤ Take with fresh seriousness the message of unity in the Spirit, within its own borders as well as beyond.
> ➤ Move "the Bible is our only creed" from its position of group slogan to a functioning reality, taking Bible study and proclamation much more seriously.
> ➤ Stop passing General Assembly resolutions and doing major self-studies only to put them on a shelf and proceed largely unchanged.
> ➤ Take daring initiatives to activate its central theme of the fellowship of all believers across denominational lines, bridging more than judging.
> ➤ Leave its arrogant role of criticizing the Christian community for its failures, as though it now stands wholly outside the problem itself.
> ➤ Share, confidently but humbly, biblical insights it believes will be for the good of the whole church and itself (some of these are identified above).
> ➤ Get beyond thinking and acting as it did in rural Midwest America in the late nineteenth century by reaching globally and being enriched by the great diversity now present in its own twenty-first century ranks.

As the Movement's Gloria Gaither has well said, if challenges like the above are met, then "there is no group in a better position to help bring joyous reconciliation among all God's people and to spread that joy to all the precious human beings God created."[139] She has spoken eloquently about the United States as a nation, making an observation appropriate for the future of the Movement. "If we who love our great land lose our vision, our drive to keep believing that there is a dream out there for a more perfect union and an ideal that could become a reality, we will slide into the oblivion of lost nations and forgotten people."[140]

The Movement must keep its unity-in-the-Spirit dream alive and dare to envision and model this biblical ideal. One simple presentation of this dream, this identity and mission vision, was captured in the *ARISE!* theme of the 2006 "Strategic Planning Conference" of the Movement. The dream is to **A**nnounce God's good news to the world; **R**elate as God's Spirit-born children; **I**nvest for the sake of God's kingdom; **S**hare in response to God's call; and **E**mpower God's gifted people for ministry. Let us arise!

Repeating this dream and the actions that must activate and accompany it is done in the hope that today's Church of God Movement will indeed **Arise**, grasp its fresh opportunities, embrace its global constituency, and keep moving and leaning forward with courage and creativity!

God's Tents Our Home

The Church of God Movement always has understood itself as an *interim body*, a "leaven in the loaf" seeking to bring fresh health and maturation to the whole church. It has resisted the idea that it is an established religious institution in the mix of many others. It has been called to bring a positive impact to the whole and then cease to exist once this task is complete. It's been a pilgrim people journeying with God through the wilderness of this world. The biblical narrative is filled with dreams and visions reaching beyond the compromised present to a promised future.

The detail of what lies ahead is not ours to know. We live in the dim light of the already-not yet, the dawning rather than the high noon of God's realized reign. Even so, there is light. God's kingdom has been inaugurated in our human midst. His name is Jesus. The ministries of God's Spirit are present and real. The holy God still wants and intends a holy people united on mission together.

The Church of God Movement always has insisted that Christian unity is both necessary and possible if world mission is to be successful. Now many church bodies around the world are finally freed of European and North American provincialism. We live in a post-denominational environment that this Movement has called for since its beginning. A fresh frontier for the church in our time clearly is *globalization*. There is an earnest seeking worldwide for the church as it ought to be, apart from the dominance of excessive human structuring or the patterns of a given culture. Communication is now so immediate and universal that church leaders around the world can become well acquainted and strategize together as never before.

The challenge for the Movement today is to do more than theorize about a "united church for a divided world." Meaningful togetherness in Christ requires intentional initiatives. Diversities within the Movement must be better bridged. The 1984 "Consultation on Mission and Ministry" of the Movement in the United States and Canada stated an even broader goal: "We must expand ministries through voluntary relationships with groups outside the Church of God." The 1988 General Assembly approved a set of guidelines for inter-church relationships, cautioning only that all such bodies must believe in the full lordship of Jesus Christ. The many other differences among the numerous Christian church bodies must not be allowed to divide, obstruct, and distract.

Our Lord is the key to both the past and future, the necessary foundation for churchwide fellowship and common mission. He's *the* Subject! So God's people are called to travel confidently on, rallying around the Lord, becoming ever more like him, and together making the tents of God their daily home.

As God's people travel on as God guides, they must keep in mind that being a "reformation people" isn't a reality that is easily passed from generation to generation like the family Bible. There continues to be need for reformation in the church, and each generation must see and engage the particulars of this need in its time and place. Each must dare to engage freshly in the necessary battle to overcome the obstacles to the realization of God's holy, united, ministering church.

To be a "movement" is by definition a paradoxical experience. The members must have a clear understanding of who they are and what they are to be about. They are to be change agents called by God. A movement is to be an ongoing process, not an end product It's to be a quest and not a completed arrival. Its members must not be settlers but frontier people with an exploring and experimenting spirit. To be a "movement" requires staying young and visionary, willing to risk failure in repeated attempts to reach the greater good. People are not adequate for this challenge. Divine grace is definitely essential.

I attempted above a fresh mission statement for the Church of God Movement. Here's a second attempt:

> *Today's Movement is called to be a global body of visionary and vibrant Christians who have much yet to learn, much life in Christ's Spirit yet to be deepened, a series of important truth perspectives yet to be shared, and a determination to reach toward, strengthen, and serve the whole church. This Movement must see itself less as an exiled remnant of the truly faithful and more as a humble witness to the church universal, a witness aware of and intentionally living from the theological riches resident in its Wesleyan-Holiness tradition.*

Such a witness to the church universal, to be credible and effective, must come from *within* and not from *outside* everybody else in God's family. For the Movement, the witness began in the 1880s with a holy arrogance supposedly coming from outside the established church world. Now the Movement must proceed differently, chastened but not discouraged, moving forward from the inside with more of a holy humility.

There's real spiritual life to be had, holiness to be reached, a church to unite, and a world to save. Quite a challenge! Impossible? Yes, at least on our own. But Jesus himself set us on this journey and left us with his empowering Spirit. Since we are called to this challenge, and have been promised the needed grace and gifting, the Movement must come to freshly believe that the adventure is not only worthy but possible. It must dedicate itself to nothing less!

The key words are still "open" and "forward." The Church of God Movement must stay open to God, to the whole of God's family, and to today's human needs. It must dare to keep learning, growing, experimenting, relating, risking, serving, and moving forward at the nudging and with the assistance of God's Spirit. It indeed must be "a movement, a catalytic fellowship and leavening influence lifting up the essential nature of Christian unity, unity in the person, power, and love of Christ."[141]

As the Movement accepts the tents of God as its own mobile home, it should keep singing Charles W. Naylor's beloved words, "Joyful we walk on the King's highway, *forward, ever forward!*"

NEEDED CONVERSATION AND ACTION

1. Do you believe that the Church of God Movement has a particular mission among all the churches in the world today? If so, what is it? Two possibilities of mission statement are suggested in this chapter. Are they clear and appropriate? If there is no particular mission, then why does the Movement continue to exist as a church reform body?

2. Is it true that a "movement," to be true to itself, must keep moving, changing as the circumstances around it change? So much has changed in the church world since the Movement's beginning in 1880. Has the Movement adjusted appropriately? Are we still acting like it's still the nineteenth century?

3. The cooperative ministries of the Movement in the United States and Canada are led by Church of God Ministries. Is this body leading the Movement appropriately? If not, what should be done differently? Should anyone be leading other than the Holy Spirit? Does the Spirit sometimes lead through called individuals and faithful church bodies?

4. What would you like to see your state/region/provincial assembly leaders do as a next step now that you have read this book and been part of exploring its questions?

5. On the local level, what would you like to see your pastor and other congregational leaders do differently? Is there something you are being called to do personally?

6. The Church of God Movement must stay open to God, to the whole of God's family, and to today's human needs. It must dare to keep learning, growing, experimenting, relating, risking, serving, and mov-

ing forward. Will it do all of this creatively and courageously or is it resistant to change, caught in some yesterday that is no more?

7. Has this chapter or the entire book made you uncomfortable in any way? What would you like to explore more deeply? What questions have come that your family or congregation should explore? Will you see that this happens?

INTO ALL
THE WORLD

A Century of Church of God Missions

CENTENNIAL CELEBRATION

1909–2009

GLOBAL MISSIONS

LESTER A. CROSE
CHERYL JOHNSON BARTON
DONALD D. JOHNSON

APPENDIX

One way of illustrating the central concerns of the Church of God Movement is to present the following personal witness.

DON'T CALL ME "CHRISTIAN"!

The Personal Witness of Barry L. Callen

The term *Christianity* was not original with the rise of the Jesus people. It was something that appeared later in a given set of political circumstances. A Roman emperor decided around 315 A.D. that it was to his political advantage to adopt the Jesus Movement of Judaism as his very own, reducing the Jesus people to being virtual wards of the Roman Empire.

"Christianity" had been reduced to an institutionalized glue being used to help hold the Empire together. How ironic. The Jews had opposed Jesus and encouraged his crucifixion because he failed to dismantle that Empire on their behalf! Consequently, if the word "Christian" means a way to prop up any human empire, I would prefer being called something else.

Aspects of the Christian world today, and some aspects of its history, are hardly worth being associated with by a serious believer in Jesus. Indeed, it may be better for believers to be known simply as dedicated disciples of Jesus than be painted with a broader "religious" brush of a complex tradition. To take the general name "Christian" requires explaining what it's not. Adjectives usually have to be added to clarify what brand of Christian one is—liberal, fundamental, evangelical, ecumenical, pentecostal, Eastern, Western, etc. All of these adjectives have volatile histories and a series of associated meanings that are respectable and otherwise.

It also needs to be made clear that, despite the Christian past, at least I, one contemporary representative of the faith, actually opposes slavery, judges the crusades of the Middle Ages an embarrassment, and respects women as true equals in social and church life. And more, I at least respect those not accepting the divinity and lordship of Jesus, rather than reducing them to no more than mere targets of aggressive evangelism. I also recall that Jesus was a loyal Jew and his fellow Jews in any age are not to be persecuted. The "Old" Testament must not be thrown into the Christian's garbage can—as though the New Testament could be understood without it. See my book *Beneath the Surface* that attempts to end centuries of its discrediting by Christianity.

I see much merit in going back to the New Testament accounts of Jesus and focusing my faith identity directly on his actual person, recorded teachings, and amazing resurrection. Such going back seeks to relax the need to explain the "kind" of Christian I now am. I'm the kind that seeks to be Christ-like. I hope to distance myself from the terrible misdeeds of some past representatives of Christianity.

To be known simply as a follower of Jesus brings a little relief from being restricted by a given creedal or national tradition of the faith that has both its strengths and inevitable frailties. If you must label me somehow, please make the label "just one of the humble men trying to follow the Master."

The Church of God Movement for many generations has been saying much of what I'm trying to say. Denominations tend to be tribal and artificially narrowing of Christian fellowship and cooperation in mission. Formal creeds, especially when required for group membership, tend to stifle searching after the fuller truth and often encourage a destructive division among believers. Religious labels stereotype unfairly and isolate unnecessarily from brothers and sisters in the faith. They also tend to give the general public sad misconceptions of the actual truth.

So I, and generations of leaders of the Church of God Movement, have hoped to step outside this tendency to "sectism" and return to the "apostolic" foundations of the faith. We have wanted our primary identity to be sincere followers of Jesus, enabled by the wisdom and power of Christ's Spirit. We have relied on a particular name of the Jesus followers, simply the "Church of God." We have overstated the case when insisting that the New Testament mandates this phrase as the intended formal name of the church. Even so, our instinct has been correct with our concern that the church be the one *of God* and of not any religious empire or any cultural captivity of humans.

It may be that an attempt to "come out" of human captivity and "go back" to apostolic foundations is too idealistic. I resonate with how Billy Graham once responded to the question, "Do you believe in the old-time religion?" He said, "If it's old enough." He meant that we should not revert mindlessly to the faith of our parents or theirs before them. We must go clear back to the source and fountain of the faith, the New Testament and Jesus himself. This is what the Church of God Movement has meant by restoring the faith's "apostolic" roots and breaking free from centuries of church compromises and captivities.

The Movement obviously has experienced only partial success in the implementation of this vision. Even so, I judge this visionary idealism a truly good way to go. At least it keeps pointing to what God intends for the church. The church is the fellowship of Jesus and it's for all people who are deeply committed to him and being changed by the power of Christ's Spirit. It's for all who are hungering daily for a further maturing of their spiritual experience and understanding, who have been seized by a vision of all God's people as one united and living family, and who are humble enough to keep growing and learning without restricting the freedom of others to do the same.

I don't want to be known as an adherent of some "section" of Christians who sit smugly in their little corner and look critically at all others who understand differently a point or two of doctrine or practice. I want to be identified with Jesus and all his people who are reaching for the fullness of the truth that is in him. I want to keep stretching beyond the compromises of the highly institutionalized "churches" and the tragically divided Christian world.

Effective Christian evangelism requires that the church *be the church in its intended holiness and unity*. No group or movement of believers has a corner on truth. Authority lies in the biblical revelation of God in Jesus Christ, not in the interpretations and traditions of any one body of believers, including the Church of God Movement.

So, please just call me a sincere follower of Jesus on journey with the Master. As the Movement's beloved Dale Oldham put it in a song title, "Let Me See *Jesus Only*!" Jesus was none other than God with us. That's why I want my identity focused on him. I love his people, but not all they have come to represent.

The center of Christian faith is the person of Jesus Christ and renewed relationship with God through him. It's not an identifying with all the history, structures, and creeds that have carried the name "Christianity." I wish to be a citizen of the "kingdom" of God rather than of any human "empire," religious or not.[142]

BIBLIOGRAPHY
SELECT CHURCH OF GOD PUBLICATIONS

AUTOBIOGRAPHIES OF MAJOR MOVEMENT LEADERS
1. Byrum, Enoch E., *Life Experiences*, Gospel Trumpet Co., 1928.
2. Callen, Barry L., *A Pilgrim's Progress*, Anderson University Press and Emeth Press, 3ʳᵈ ed., 2019.
3. Cole, Mary, *Trials and Triumphs of Faith*, Gospel Trumpet Co., 1914.
4. Collins, Donald, *There Were Angels Along My Way: The Story of My Life As I Remember It,* published privately, 2010.
5. Gray, Albert F., *Time and Tides on the Western Shore*, pub. privately, 1966.
6. Jeeninga, Gustav, *Doors to Life: The Stories of Jeeninga*, Anderson University Press, 2002.
7. Krenz, Willi, *Always Looking Forward*, Anderson University Press, 2010.
8. Massey, James Earl, *Aspects of My Pilgrimage*, Anderson University Press, 2002.
9. Morrison, John A., *As the River Flows*, Anderson College Press, 1962.
10. Nicholson, Robert A., *So I Said, Yes!*, Anderson University Press, 2006.
11. Newberry, Gene W., *A Boy from Lewis County*, published privately, 2000.
12. Oldham, W. Dale, *Giants Along My Path*, Warner Press, 1973.
13. Pistole, Hollis, *My Story: A Personal Account of Some Fascinating Trails by a Very Fortunate Traveler*, Chinaberry House, 2004.
14. Reardon, Robert H., *This Is the Way It Was*, Warner Press, 1991.

BIOGRAPHIES OF MAJOR MOVEMENT LEADERS
1. Bolitho, Axchie, *To the Chief Singer* (Barney E. Warren), Gospel Trumpet Co., 1942.
2. Byers, Andrew L., *Birth of a Reformation* (Daniel S. Warner), Gospel Trumpet Co., 1921.
3. Byrum, Noah H., *Familiar Names and Faces*, Gospel Trumpet Company, 1902.

4. Callen, Barry L., *It's God's Church!* (Daniel S. Warner), Warner Press, 1995.
5._____. *She Came Preaching* (Lillie S. McCutcheon), Warner Press, 1992.
6._____. ed., *The Wisdom of the Saints*, Life Sketches of Thirty Leaders, Anderson University Press and Warner Press, 2003.
7._____. *Staying on Course* (Robert H. Reardon), Anderson University Press, 2004.
8. Hawkins, Mary Ann, Juanita Evans Leonard, eds., *A Thread of Hope: Church of God Women in Mission*, Anderson University Press, 2009.
9. Heffren, Henry C., *Voices of the Pioneers,* published privately, 1968.
10. Ludwig, Charles, *A Dangerous Obedience* (J. Horace Germany), Warner Press, 1994.
11. Massey, James Earl, *Raymond S. Jackson*, Warner Press, 1967.
12. Neal, Hazel, Axchie Bolitho, *Madam President* (Nora Hunter), Warner Press, 1982.
13. Newell, Arlo F., *A Servant in God's Kingdom* (Max Gaulke), Warner Press, 1995.
14. Welch, Douglas E., *Ahead of His Times* (George P. Tasker), Anderson University Press, 2001.

HISTORIES OF THE CHURCH OF GOD MOVEMENT

1. Brown, Charles E., *When the Trumpet Sounded*, Warner Press, 1951.
2._____. *When Souls Awaken*, Gospel Trumpet Co, 1954.
3. Callen,, Barry L. *A Time to Remember* (six paperbacks), Warner Press, 1977-1978.
4._____. *The First Century*, 2 vols., Warner Press, 1979.
5._____. *Radical Christianity*, Evangel Press, 1999.
6._____. ed., *Following the Light*, Warner Press, 2000.
7._____. *Seeking Higher Ground* (Park Place Church of God, Anderson, IN), Park Place Church, 2006.
8._____.Callen, Barry L., *Enriching Mind and Spirit*, higher education, Anderson University Press, 2007.
9._____.Callen, Barry L., *Leaning Forward*, General Assembly, Emeth Press, 2019.
10. Clear, Val. B., *Where the Saints Have Trod*, Midwest Publications, 1977.
11. Crose, Lester A., *Passport for a Reformation*, Warner Press, 1981.

12. Crose, Lester, Cheryl Johnson Barton, Donald Johnson, *Into All the World*, Warner Press, 2009.
13. Massey, James Earl, *African-Americans and the Church of God*, Anderson University Press, 2005.
14. Phillips, Harold L., *Miracle of Survival*, Warner Press, 1979.
15. Reardon, Robert H., *The Early Morning Light*, Warner Press, 1979.
16. Riggle, Herbert M., *Pioneer Evangelism*, Gospel Trumpet Co., 1924.
17. Smith, John W. V., *A Brief History of the Church of God Movement*, Warner Press, 1976.
18. Smith, John W. V., *The Quest for Holiness and Unity*, Warner Press, 1980, rev. ed., 2009.
19. Strege, Merle D., *I Saw the Church*, Warner Press, 2002.
20. Strege, Merle D., *The Desk As Altar: The Centennial History of Anderson University*, Anderson University Press, 2016.
21. Warner, Daniel S., and H. M. Riggle, *The Cleansing of the Sanctuary*, Gospel Trumpet Co., 1903.
22. Wickersham, Henry C., *A History of the Church*, Gospel Trumpet Co., 1900.

THEOLOGIES BY CHURCH OF GOD SCHOLARS

1. Brown, Charles E., *The Apostolic Church*, Warner Press, 1947.
2. Byrum, Russell R., *Christian Theology*, Gospel Trumpet Co., 1925.
3. Callen, Barry L., *God As Loving Grace*, Evangel Pub., 1996, Wipf & Stock, 2018.
4. _____. *Contours of a Cause*, Anderson School of Theology, 1995.
5. _____. *Discerning the Divine*, Westminster/John Knox, 2004.
6. _____. *Caught Between Truths*, Emeth Press, 2007.
7. _____. *Approaching Theology*, Emeth Press, 2015.
8. _____. *Heart of the Matter*, Emeth Press, 2011, rev. ed., 2016.
9. Gray, Albert F., *Christian Theology*, 2 vols., Warner Press, 1944-1946.
10. Jones, Kenneth, *Theology of Holiness and Love*, University Press of America, 1995.
11. Martin, Earl L., *Toward Understanding God*, Gospel Trumpet Publishing Co., 1942.
12. Miller, Gene, ed., *Dynamics of the Faith*, Gulf-Coast Bible College, 1972.
13. Sanders, Cliff, *The Optimism of Grace*, MACU Press, 2016.

14. Smith, F. G., *What the Bible Teaches*, Gospel Trumpet Publishing Co., 1914. Condensed by Kenneth Jones, 1955.

15. Smith, John W. V., *I Will Build My Church: Biblical Insights on Distinguishing Doctrines of the Church of God*, Warner Press, 1999.

16. Stafford, Gilbert W., *Theology for Disciples*, Warner Press, 1996, 2012.

ACADEMIC DISSERTATIONS ABOUT THE CHURCH OF GOD

1. Callen, Barry L., "Church of God Movement: A Study in Ecumenical Idealism," Asbury Theological Seminary, 1969.

2. Clear, Val B., "The Church of God: A Study in Social Adaptation," University of Chicago, 1953. Published as *Where the Saints Have Trod* (Midwest Publications, 1977).

3. Collins, Donald L., "Sin and Obedience in the Life of the Christian," Union Theological Seminary, 1957.

4. Hartman, Marvin J., "The Origin and Development of the General Ministerial Assembly of the Church of God," Butler University, 1958.

5. Forrest, Aubrey Leland, "A Study of the Development of the asic Doctrines and Institutional Patterns in the Church of God," University of Southern California, 1948.

6. O'Brien, Glen, "North American Wesleyan-Holiness Churches in Australia," LaTrobe University, 2005.

7. Preston, Lee Dean, "Charles E. Brown: His Life and Influence on the Organization of the Life and Work of the Church of God (Anderson, IN)," Iliff School of Theology, 1969.

8. Reardon, Robert H., "The Doctrine of the Church and Christian Life in the Church of God Reformation Movement," Oberlin Graduate School of Theology, 1943.

9. Smith, John W. V., "The Approach of the Church of God (Anderson, IN) and Comparable Groups to the Problem of Christian Unity," University of Southern California, 1954.

10. Stafford, Gilbert W., "Experiential Salvation and Christian Unity in the Thought of Seven Theologians of the Church of God (Anderson, IN)," Boston University School of Theology, 1973.

THE BIBLE

1. Blackwelder, Boyce W., *Light from the Greek New Testament*, Baker Book House, 1976.

2. Callen, Barry L., ed. *Listening to the Word of God*, honoring Boyce Blackwelder, Warner Press, 1990.
3.____ with Richard Thompson, *Bible Reading in Wesleyan Ways*, Beacon Hill Press of Kansas City, 2004.
4.____ with Clark Pinnock, *The Scripture Principle*, Baker Academic, 2006; third edition, Emeth Press, 2009.
5.____. *Beneath the Surface*, the Old Testament, Emeth Press, 2012.
6.____. *Bible Stories for Strong Stomachs*, Cascade Books, Wipf & Stock, 2017.
7. Jones, Kenneth, *The Word of God*, Warner Press, 1980.
8. Linn, Otto F., *Studies in the New Testament*, 3 vols., Gospel Trumpet Co., 1941-42.
9. Miller, Adam W., *An Introduction to the New Testament*, Gospel Trumpet Co., 1943.

CHRISTIAN HOLINESS

1. Brown, Charles E., *The Meaning of Sanctification*, Warner Press, 1945.
2. Callen, Barry L., *The Prayer of Holiness-Hungry People*: Guide to the Lord's Prayer, Francis Asbury Press, 2011.
3.____ with Don Thorsen, eds., *Heart & Life*: Rediscovering Holy Living, Aldersgate Press, 2012.
4.____. *Catch Your Breath!*: Exhaling Death and Inhaling Life, Aldersgate Press, 2014.
5.____. *Color Me Holy*: Holy God, Holy People, with Hubert Harriman, Aldersgate Press, 2013, 2015.
6. Jones, Kenneth, *Commitment to Holiness*, Warner Press, 1985.
7. Newell, Arlo F., *Receive the Holy Spirit*, Warner Press, 1978.
8. Warner, Daniel S., *Bible Proofs of the Second Work of Grace*, Mennonite Pub. Society, 1880.

CHRISTIAN UNITY

1. Brown, Charles E., *A New Approach to Christian Unity*, Gospel Trumpet Co., 1931.
2. Brown, Charles E., *The Church Beyond Division*, Gospel Trumpet Co., 1939.
3. Callen, Barry L., with James North, *Coming Together in Christ*, College Press Pub. Co., 1997.

4._____. ed., *The Holy River of God*, Aldersgate Press, 2016.

5. Massey, James Earl, *Concerning Christian Unity*, Warner Press, 1979.

ESCHATOLOGY

1. Callen, Barry L., *Faithful in the Meantime*, Evangel Publishing House, 1997, reprint 2018 by Wipf & Stock.

2. Dwyer, Timothy, *On the Street Level: The Scroll of the Apocalypse* (Free Methodist Publishing House, Light and Life), forthcoming 2020.

3. Gaulke, Max, *Thy Kingdom Come—Now!*, Warner Press, 1959.

4. Linn, Otto F., *Studies in the New Testament*, 3 vols., Gospel Trumpet Co., 1941-42.

5. Miller, Adam W., *An Introduction to the New Testament*, Gospel Trumpet Co., 1943.

6. McCutcheon, Lillie S., *The Symbols Speak* (Warner Press, 1992).

7. Riggle, Herbert M., *Christ's Kingdom and Reign*, Gospel Trumpet Co., 1918.

8. Schell, William G., *The Biblical Trace of the Church*, Gospel Trumpet Co., 1893.

9. Smith, Frederick G., *The Revelation Explained*, Gospel Trumpet Co., 1908 and various later editions.

10. Strong, Marie, *Basic Teachings from Patmos* (Warner Press, 1980, rev. 1995).

ACKNOWLEDGMENTS

I love the church body about which I write. I both look back with gratitude and analyze without apology the journey of the Church of God Movement, both the very good and sometimes the not so good. I do this to identify ways the Movement can face a new future with fresh vision and effectiveness. It deserves to be enriched by its exceptional past and must be willing to make necessary adjustments. Some things have not stood the test of time.

I follow the direction of Proverbs 19:20. I'm very willing to take good counsel. No work of this kind could be done without the shared wisdom of many hearts and minds, past and present. I'm deeply in their debt. The many endnotes of this book highlight those persons and publications from the past that have informed me with their considerable wisdom.

I also have gladly turned to present leaders of the Movement for guidance and wisdom. In particular, I acknowledge Jeannette Flynn, a lifelong friend. She provided critical inspiration and practical assistance to my work. Thank you, Jeannette! And thanks to Jan, my wonderful wife, who skillfully proofed the final manuscript.

In addition, and with Jeannette's assistance, I turned to a series of diverse leaders of today's Movement, seeking their candid critiques of this evolving work. Their questions, concerns, and suggestions combined to make these pages better than otherwise they would have been. Even so, any remaining weakness certainly is not their responsibility. Several of them offered generous endorsement statements that appear on the back cover and elsewhere.

I wish to name some of these consultants with my sincere gratitude. They are: Darryl O. Allen, Joe Allison, David Aukerman, John H. Aukerman, Bernie Barton, Ryan Chapman, Donald L. Collins, Curtiss DeYoung, Ronald V. Duncan, Ronald J. Fowler, Mark Andrew Gale, Jerry C. Grubbs, Steve Hency, Donald D. Johnson, Arthur M. Kelly, Philip L. Kinley, Rainer Klinner, Andre Machel, Marshall Lawrence, Scott Lewis, Robert L. Moss, C. D. Oliver, Robert W. Pearson, Melissa Pratt, J. David and Greta Reames, Gerald Rudd, Cliff D. Sanders, Sieg Schuler, Ruben Schwieger, Mark Shaner, Joy Sherman, Fredrick Shively, Ann E. Smith,

Paul Strozier, Jason Varner, and Nathan Willowby. In addition are the numerous women and men of yesterday and today whose writings I have consulted and often quoted (see the endnotes). This representative list of names includes many of the Movement's leading editors, historians, theologians, executives, and educators. I and this book are in their debt.

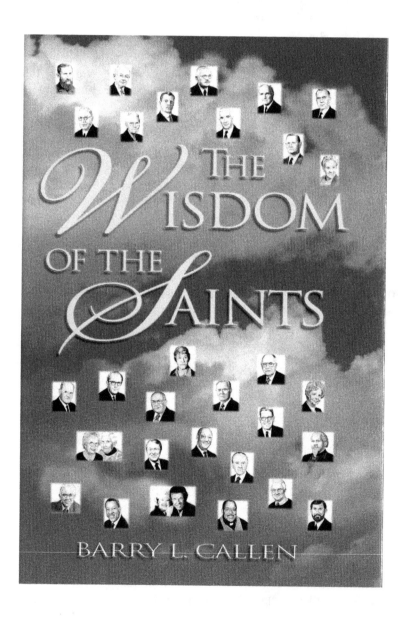

ENDNOTES

1. Barry L. Callen, in his Foreword to Charles E. Brown, *The Meaning of Sanctification*, Gospel Trumpet Co., 1945, reissued with the new Foreword in 2013 by Francis Asbury Press.

2. Tod Bolsinger, *Canoeing the Mountains: Christian Leadership in Uncharted Territory* (IVP Books), 41.

3. Walter Brueggemann, "A Dangerous Oddness," in *Sojourners*, January, 2020, 26. By "prophetic" he means that "prophets are able to imagine the world other than the way it is in front of them...and then articulate the alternative world that God has promised and is birthing."

4. Russell R. Byrum, 1928, in Barry L. Callen, *The First Century*, vol. 2 (Warner Press, 1979), 42.

5. Albert F. Gray, in the *Gospel Trumpet*, Jan. 7, 1950.

6. Gray's particular criticisms of the thinking and acting of the "early brethren" included their wrong expectation of the soon return of Christ, indulging in the appeal to biblical prophecy to support the Movement's identity and mission, their extreme anti-organization attitude, and their tendency to "demand a uniformity of doctrine and practice which went beyond that required by the Bible."

7. This provocative phrase has meanings in the present unrelated to its use in the early generations of Church of God people. For them, and in this writing, it has to do with leaving church bodies judged apostate and abandoned by God.

8. Barry Callen graduated from Asbury Theological Seminary in 1969 and was honored by that seminary in 2019 as a "golden grad."

9. William Barclay, *The Gospel of Matthew*, 1975, 7.

10. Robert H. Reardon, *The Early Morning Light* (Warner Press, 1979), 96.

11. Warner's full personal story is recounted in Barry L. Callen, *It's God's Church!* (Warner Press, 1995).

12. Explored extensively in Barry Callen's master's thesis at Asbury Theological Seminary (1969), the Church of God began as an exercise in "ecumenical idealism."

13. Church historian Merle D. Strege, in his 2002 *I Saw the Church*, explains in detail how this "prophetic" addition came about.

14. Barry L. Callen, *It's God's Church!* (Warner Press, 1995).

15. Daniel S. Warner and Herbert M. Riggle, *The Cleansing of the Sanctuary* (Gospel Trumpet Co., 1903).

16. Harold L. Phillips, *Wisdom for the Church* (Warner Press, 2006).

17. Barry L. Callen, ed., *The Church that God Intends* (Emeth Press, 2009), 6.

18. See Barry Callen's biography of Daniel Warner, *It's God's Church!* (Warner Press, 1995).

19. Daniel Warner and H. M. Riggle, *The Cleansing of the Sanctuary*, 266.

20. See Barry Callen's 1969 masters thesis at Asbury Theological Seminary that details the troubled relationship between the early Church of God Movement and the Free Methodist Church.

21. Val Clear, *Where the Saints Have Trod* (Midwest Publications, 1977), 3.

22. Robert H. Reardon, *The Way It Was* (Warner Press, 1991), 60-61.

23. Barry L. Callen, *She Came Preaching* (Warner Press, 1992).

24. See her *The Symbols Speak* (published privately, 1964, revised, Reformation Publishers, 1999).

25. H. M. Riggle, *Pioneer Evangelism* (Gospel Trumpet Co., 1924).

26. As quoted in son Robert Reardon's book *The Early Morning Light* (Warner Press, 1979), 55-56.

27. See the popular book of Lillie McCutcheon, *The Symbols Speak*. I authored her biography, *She Came Preaching* (Warner Press, 1992) out of great respect for her person and pastoral ministry, if not her manner of interpreting the Book of Revelation.

28. Charles E. Brown, *When the Trumpet Sounded* (Warner Press, 1951), 353.

29. See Brown's *When Souls Awaken* (Warner Press, 1954) and the expansion of this historical perspective in Barry L. Callen, *Radical Christianity* (Evangel Publishing, 1999).

30. Housed in the Archives of the Church of God Movement on the Anderson University campus is Warner's copy of Uriah Smith's commentary on the Book of Revelation. It includes Warner's handwritten marginal notes.

31. .Merle D. Strege, *I Saw the Church* (Warner Press, 2002), 216.

32. Marie Strong, *Basic Teachings from Patmos* (Warner Press, 1980, rev. and expanded in 1995 under the new title *A Commonsense Approach to the Book of Revelation*).

33. Timothy Dwyer, *On the Street Level: The Scroll of the Apocalypse* (Free Methodist Publishing House, Light and Life), forthcoming 2020.

34. Otto F. Linn, *Studies in the New Testament*, 1942, vol. 3.

35. Howard A. Snyder, *The Radical Wesley* (Seedbed Publishing, 2014), 145-148.

36. For detail on this critical time of testing of the school, see Barry L. Callen, *Guide of Soul and Mind* (Anderson University and Warner Press, 1992). Ongoing is the question of "Church of God doctrine." Is there such a thing? Should there be?

37. Strege, *I Saw the Church*, 198.

38. Robert H. Reardon's reflections offered to the Board of Trustees of Anderson University on the occasion of his retirement as president, April, 1983.

39. Major academic studies detailing this emerging new reality were by Val B. Clear, Leland Forrest, Robert H. Reardon, and John W. V. Smith. See detail in the Bibliography above. The dissertation by Glen O'Brien reports that this

move from "sect" to "church" hardly happened for the Church of God Movement in Australia.

40. Merle D. Strege, *I Saw the Church*, 314.

41. For a detailed sampling of this range of issues and the Movement's attitudes toward them, see the resolutions of the General Assembly in Barry L. Callen, *Leaning Forward* (Emeth Press, 2019).

42. Val Clear, "Reflections of a Postsectarian," in *The Christian Century*, January 16, 1963, 74.

43. Barry L. Callen, *It's God's Church!* (Warner Press, 1995).

44. John W. V. Smith, *The Quest for Holiness and Unity* (Warner Press, 1980, 2009), 516.

45. Robert H. Reardon, *The Early Morning Light*, 87.

46. Address by Dr. Jeffrey Frymire to the 2019 General Assembly of the Church of God in Orlando, Florida, June, 2019.

47. Philip L. Kinley, in Barry Callen, ed., *A Time To Remember: Projections* (Warner Press, 1978), 70-71.

48. See these resolutions in Barry L. Callen, *Leaning Forward* (Emeth Press, 2019).

49. James Earl Massey, *African-Americans and the Church of God* (Anderson University Press, 2005).

50. Barry L. Callen, "The Precarious Church Paradox and the National Association of the Church of God," in the *Wesleyan Theological Journal* (53:1, 2018).

51. John W. V. Smith, *Heralds of a Brighter Day* (Gospel Trumpet Co., 1955), 125.

52. Study found in MaryAnn Hawkins, general editor, *Called to Minister, Empowered to Serve*, 2 ed. (Warner Press, 2013). See also Randal Huber, *Called, Equipped, and No Place To Go: Women Pastors and the Church of God* (Warner Press, 2003).

53. Lillie S. McCutcheon, in *Vital Christianity* (May, 1989).

54. Sharon Clark Pearson, in Barry Callen and Richard Thompson, eds., *Bible Reading in Wesleyan Ways* (Beacon Hill Press of Kansas City, 2004), 188-215. For the Church of God position and experiences in particular, see MaryAnn Hawkins, general editor, *Called to Minister, Empowered to Serve, 2 ed.* (Warner Press, 2013).

55. This conflict has surfaced in various periods of the history of the school, including a cautionary resolution of the General Assembly in 1918. For the full story, see Barry L. Callen, *Guide of Soul and Mind*: The Story of Anderson University (Anderson University and Warner Press, 1992). Also see Merle D. Strege, *The Desk As Altar*, Anderson University Press, 2016.

56. The full story of each of these schools is found in Barry L. Callen, *Enriching Mind and Spirit* (Anderson University Press, 2007).

57. Harold Phillips, *Miracle of Survival* (Warner Press, 1979).

58. See Barry L. Callen, *Leaning Forward!* (2019) for the content of all related resolutions by the General Assembly.

59. For a good example, see W. Dale Oldham, *Giants Along My Path* (Warner Press, 1973), 213-214.

60. For a comprehensive presentation of all the General Assembly actions, see Barry L. Callen, *Leaning Forward!* (2019).

61. The letter graphically criticized an aspect of the Social Work curriculum of Anderson University because of what the minister judged excessive sexual explicitness.

62. For detail, see Barry L. Callen's 2019 book *Leaning Forward*.

63. Many of these saints of the distant and recent past are found in Noah H. Byrum's *Familiar Names and Faces* (Gospel Trumpet Co., 1902) and in Barry L. Callen's *The Wisdom of the Saints* (Anderson University Press and Warner Press, 2003).

64. Gilbert W. Stafford, *Theology for Disciples* (Warner Press, 1996, 2012), 35.

65. Merle D. Strege, *I Saw the Church*, 225, 227.

66. See Barry L. Callen, *Heart of the Matter: Frank Conversations among Great Christian Thinkers on the Major Subjects of Christian Theology* (Emeth Press, 2011, rev. ed., 2016), especially the references throughout to the significant work of Thomas C. Oden.

67. Merle D. Strege, *I Saw the Church*, 267.

68. Barry L. Callen and Clark H. Pinnock, *The Scripture Principle*, 3 ed. (Emeth Press, 2009), 11.

69. Barry L. Callen and Richard P. Thompson, eds., *Reading the Bible in Wesleyan Ways* (Beacon Hill Press of Kansas City, 2004), 64-65.

70. See especially M. Robert Mulholland, Jr., *Shaped by the Word*: The Power of Scripture in Spiritual Formation (rev. ed., Upper Room Books, 2000).

71. Merle D. Strege, in Barry Callen, ed., *The Church that God Intends* (Emeth Press, 2009), 238.

72. Merle D. Strege, "Building a Young Reformation Movement," in Barry Callen, ed., *The Church that God Intends*, 78.

73. All-Boards Congress of the Church of God, 1963. For detail, see Barry L. Callen, *Leaning Forward* (2019).

74. For detail, see Barry L. Callen, *Contours of the Cause* (Anderson University School of Theology, 1995), chapter 1. The early Movement was influenced strongly by at least five theological traditions of Christianity—Lutheran, Reformed, Pietist, Wesleyan, and Anabaptist (Believers Church).

75. F. G. Smith, *Brief Sketch of the Origin, Growth, and Distinctive Doctrines of Church of God Reformation Movement*, Gospel Trumpet Co., 1927.

76. Lillie McCutcheon was ordained in 1947 with the prayerful hands of F. G. Smith on her shoulders. She later reported, "That prayer may have been the time that a gift of prophecy was given to me." See her biography, *She Came

Preaching (Barry Callen, Warner Press, 1992), 108.

77. Barry Callen, *Contours of a Cause*, 44.

78. Barry Callen, *Contours of a Cause*, 196, 204-05.

79. Robert H. Reardon, *The Early Morning Light*, 42.

80. John W. V. Smith, *The Quest for Holiness and Unity*, 1980, 88-94.

81. Arlo F. Newell, in Barry Callen, *The First Century*, vol. 2, Warner Press, 1979, 38.

82. For a fuller presentation of how best to approach the doing of Christian theology, see Barry L. Callen, *Approaching Theology*, Emeth Press, 2015.

83. Note the books by Earl L. Martin, *Toward Understanding God*, Gospel Trumpet Publishing Co., 1942, and Barry L. Callen, *Discerning the Divine: God Through Christian Eyes*, Westminster/John Knox, 2004.

84. The theology volume *God As Loving Grace* by Barry L. Callen, Evangel Publishing House, 1996, reprint 2018 by Wipf & Stock, is organized around this very Trinitatian scheme.

85. My wife and I were privileged to be present at Wesley's Chapel in London, England, as it celebrated in 2019 its 241 anniversary as a congregation. Rev. John Wesley was the first pastor, with a more recent one, Rev. Leslie Griffiths, the honored guest preacher. He said, "as my life's years have become more numerous, the number of my sure beliefs has grown smaller. The one that clearly remains is the divine person And redeeming work of Jesus Christ."

86. Recall these early words in the Gospel of John—"the Word was made flesh and dwelt among us." This has been called the greatest single verse in the New Testament. Actually, this verse "is the New Testament because it sums up all that the New Testament seeks to say" (J. Ellsworth Kalas, *The Scriptures Sing of Christmas*, 2004, p. 57). Jesus, God with us, is the Subject!

87. Clark H. Pinnock, *Flame of Love*, InterVarsity Press, 1996, 157.

88. Richard Rohr, *On the Threshold of Transformation*, Loyola Press, 2010, xvii.

89. See Hubert P. Harriman and Barry L. Callen, *Color Me Holy*, Aldersgate Press, 2013.

90. Barry L. Callen, *The Prayer of Holiness-Hungry People*, Francis Asbury Press, 2011, audio edition, 2019, 46.

91. John W. V. Smith, *The Quest for Holiness and Unity*, Warner Press, 1980, 2009.

92. Hubert P. Harriman and Barry L. Callen, *Color Me Holy*, 83.

93. Barry L. Callen, *Contours of a Cause*, 58.

94. Kenneth Jones, *Commitment to Holiness*, Warner Press, 1985, chap. 1.

95. Barry L. Callen, *The Prayer of Holiness-Hungry People*, 17.

96. Long, Thomas G., in *Connections*: Year C, Vol. 3, A Lectionary Commentary for Preaching and Worship, Presbyterian Publishing, 116.

97. Barry L. Callen, *Catch Your Breath!*, Aldersgate Press, 2014, viii.

98. To be fair to Daniel Warner, there is evidence that in his later life he tem-

pered or actually changed his views on sanctification, education, and healing. This openness to change should help current leaders of the Movement be humble about their present understandings of various matters of theology and practice.

99. Frederick Coutts, as quoted in Jonathan Raymond, *Social Holiness*, Aldersgae Press and Crest Books, 2018, 20.

100. Verse one of the hymn "More Like Christ," in the hymnal *Worship the Lord*, Warner Press, 1989, 496. Lyrics by Charles W. Naylor.

101. R. Eugene Sterner, in Barry Callen, *The First Century*, Warner Press, 1979, 80.

102. For much of Massey's inspired writing in this regard, see *Views from the Mountain*, Callen and DeYoung, eds., Aldersgate Press, 2018;

103. T. Franklin Miller, in Barry Callen, *The First Century*, 81-82.

104. James Earl Massey, in Barry Callen, ed., *A Time To Remember: Projections*, Warner Press, 1978, 54.

105. Gilbert W. Stafford, "Holiness Church Participation in the Larger Church," in Barry Callen, ed., *The Church that God Intends*, 259-272.

106. Barry L. Callen, *Radical Christianity: The Believers Church Tradition in Christianity's History and Future*, Evangel Publishing House, 1999.

107. See the significant volume *The Holy River of God: Currents and Contributions of the Wesleyan Holiness Stream of Christianity*, Aldersgate Press, 2016, Barry Callen, editor, in which these participating denominations are identified and their commonly affirmed "Holiness Manifesto" is found.

108. Barry Callen and James North, *Coming Together in Christ*, College Press Publishing, 1997, 12.

109. See Barry L. Callen's edited books, *Sharing Heaven's Music* (1995) and *Views from the Mountain* (2018).

110. See the comprehensive history of Church of God missions in Lester Crose and others, *Into All the World*, Warner Press, 2009.

111. All-Boards Congress of the Church of God, 1963.

112. See Barry L. Callen, *Caught Between Truths: The Central Paradoxes of Christian Faith*, Emeth Press, 2007.

113. When the beloved Church of God pastor and radio speaker Dale Oldham was first contacted about coming to Anderson, Indiana, to assume a prominent role with high national visibility in the Church of God Movement, this was his response. "To criticize its leaders is one of Christianity's favorite indoor sports. Men at 'headquarters' are always the targets for the potshots of every Tom, Dick, and Harry across the nation and around the world." With a particularly strong sense of "independency," such an unfortunate tendency has been especially strong in this Movement. Oldham's comment comes from his 1973 autobiography, *Giants Along My Path*, pp. 229-230.

114. E. Stanley Jones, *A Song of Ascents*, Abingdon Press, 1968, 233.

115. Written in 1955 by Church of God missionary John D. Crose in an open letter to other missionaries in Korea.

116. Found in an email letter to Dr. Callen from Dr. Duncan, December 28, 2019, in response to a draft of this book manuscript.

117. Gilbert W. Stafford, *Theology for Disciples*, 162.

118. Howard A. Snyder, *The Radical Wesley*, Seedbed Publishing, 2014, 167.

119. Leith Anderson, "Movement for the 21 Century," April, 1996.

120. Strege, *I Saw the Church*, 289.

121. Robert Reardon, *The Early Morning Light*, 30, 38.

122. Gilbert W. Stafford, *Theology for Disciples*, 162.

123. Barry L. Callen, *It's God's Church!: The Life and Legacy of Daniel S. Warner*, Warner Press, 1995.

124. For the detail of this dramatic story, see Barry Callen's biography of Daniel Warner, *It's God's Church!*

125. Jim Lyon, General Director of Church of God Ministries, posted in *CHOG News*, September 25, 2019.

126. Richard Rohr, *On the Threshold of Transformation*, 137.

127. Timothy Dwyer, "The Day of the Lord," in *Light and Life* magazine of the Free Methodist Church, October, 2019.

128. Merle D. Strege, in Barry Callen, ed., *The Church that God Intends*, 238.

129. Barry L. Callen, *Faithful in the Meantime: A Biblical View of Final Things and Present Responsibilities*, Evangel Publishing House, 1997, Wipf & Stock, 2018, 13.

130. All General Assembly resolutions are recorded in Barry Callen, *Leaning Forward*, Emeth Press, 2019.

131. Consult the 1997 book by Barry Callen, *Faithful in the Meantime*.

132. Barry L. Callen, *Caught Between Truths: The Central Paradoxes of Christian Faith*, Emeth Press, 2007, 128.

133. Barry L. Callen, *The Prayer of Holiness-Hungry People*, 72.

134. Val Clear, *Where the Saints Have Trod*, 41-42.

135. *The Top Ten: Why Daniel Warner is Still Relevant for You and Your Church*, by Barry L. Callen, Anderson University Press, n.d.

136. Barry L. Callen, ed., *The Church that God Intends*.

137. H. M. Riggle, *Pioneer Evangelism*, Gospel Trumpet Co., 1924, 80.

138. Gilbert W. Stafford, *Church of God at the Crossroads*, Warner Press, 2000, 15, 18.

139. Gloria Gaither, in the *Saturday Evening Post*, Nov. 1985, 101.

140. From Gloria Gaither's blog, "The Alabaster City," June 27, 2019.

141. R. Eugene Sterner, in Barry Callen, ed., *A Time To Remember: Projections*, Warner Press, 1978, 81.

142. An earlier version of this essay is found in the autobiography of Barry L. Callen, *A Pilgrim's Progress*, Anderson University Press and Emeth Press, 3rd edition, 2019.